EVERYTHING ELSE INCLUDED

BY

STANLEY R. FROM

Bloomington, IN  Milton Keynes, UK

authorHOUSE®

AuthorHouse™
1663 Liberty Drive, Suite 200
Bloomington, IN 47403
www.authorhouse.com
Phone: 1-800-839-8640

AuthorHouse™ UK Ltd.
500 Avebury Boulevard
Central Milton Keynes, MK9 2BE
www.authorhouse.co.uk
Phone: 08001974150

First published by AuthorHouse 5/1/2007

ISBN: 978-1-4259-9106-7 (sc)

Printed in the United States of America
Bloomington, Indiana

This book is printed on acid-free paper.

Dedication

To Myrta whose many sincere random acts of kindness
on my behalf were greatly appreciated.

Foreword

This collection of poems is a reflection of experiences taken from a lifetime of memories; from my youth to the present day; memories mixed together with recent experiences to reflect again a journey spanning six decades of development.

Reluctantly accepting the bitter with the sweet I gradually came to realize I was a much stronger person than I gave myself credit for.

Everything Else Included is a collection of poetry dedicated to those average people who are taken for granted by their peers whose absence from the stage of every day life would cause confusion, aggrevation, and upheaval. Consistency is a behavioral mode many people do not really appreciate enough. This character trait only comes to the forefront when its disappearance is felt for the first time.

Readers: Sit back in your easy chair and prepare yourself for a journey of discovery, reflection, and fulfillment.

TABLE OF CONTENTS

A Few Good Men

The pouch hanging over his belt buckle he claims as his own
Likewise the empty playground above his eyes where grass long ago began to grow
Always a loner when witnessed on sight
Secretly wishing for female companionship to make it through another lonely night.

The evil look makes the brave connecting few hesitate then run away
The pain of an unhappy childhood makes him present himself this way
In need of guidance and support plus a few additional presents too
A strong sympathetic woman the only tonic for him so true.

A smart lawyer in the courtroom brought him down to his knees
In his longest hour of desperation there was a settlement to please
He gave the relationship his all yet others still did not understand
Is a trusting patient soul available for this trusting scar filled man?

A continuing journey to place flowers upon her grave
Upon her sudden passing he made every gallant effort to appear composed and brave
Now sunny weekend afternoons are spent taking memory walks in the park
A soft concerned voice of understanding may give his life a new spark.

Bound for life in a wheelchair after a tour of duty for Uncle Sam
These tragedies would happen to others in places like Iraq and Vietnam
Smiling after months of rehab in a medical facility far removed from the local scene
Soul searching and commitment so necessary for the formation of a new team.

Philamenia's Final Day

Eyes of anticipation signifying farewell on that final day
Taken by surprise there wasn't much for me to say
Picking up baskets other customers watched her running around
In the future removed from her favorite vocational playground.

Standing on tippitoes to reach something off a high shelf
Behind the customer service counter always worried about others instead of herself
Displaying great patience when under siege from the mother and son team
Never losing her groove always operating under a positive beam.

Finding a replacement a real challenge for this neighborhood convenience store
In the food business with competitors always going to war
In the future memories will have to satisfy pleasant thoughts about her
For the profit making drink of success a replacement will learn how to make a positive stir.

THIRTY MINUTES OF ISOLATION

The appearance of hunger from her work station drove her away
Food Pilgrims in the parking lot to the sign on the door not ready to obey
The birth of an anger salvo came forth in the middle of the night
Time to advise the Store Patriots on the inside to get things right.

Hunger, inclement weather, and the passing of time affect one and all
The decision on this issue is really a tough call
Both sides say their needs have to be met
Both sides with habit forming tendencies appear to be set.

Smiles and angry words the results of the round
The winner and the vanquished appreciate the other one's coming around
A matter of principle where no one can accept anything but the reality at hand
Sellers and consumers together at last one happy band.

BREAK TIME

A large metropolis ready for me and my buffing machine
Eliminating surface dirt in the hope of making the surface gleam
Yellow tape ready to construct boundaries throughout the many aisles
Hearing the cries of the customers with no access acting like a child.

My pay is small though the moon shines brightly outside
I keep pushing as the main virtue of my personal pride
Watching the old man searching for his favorite donuts again
If he wasn't so old I could call him my friend.

Sitting in the drug aisle I settle into conversation
What's going on at home along with news of my adopted great nation
Soon the bell will ring and my restful moments will fade into the past
No idea yet how to make the shining surface on my playground last.

SMALL BODY / LARGE SHADOW

Arriving in this country via Ellis Island as many others came
Driven to make his mark though among peers not feeling quite the same
Using verbal force to make others see his point of view
A presence of one rarely giving others their just do.

To those when in trouble knowing when to intercede
Looked upon as an expert ready to fulfill your every need
Showing off a voice of contentment when viewing the plaques upon the wall
The notes upon the report card having no use for you at all.

Mandatory training set up to help him mellow out
Even with a lower voice still retaining most of his original clout
Stressful situations now cause his system to rebel asking why
Between visits to the local doctor the days keep passing by..

SECOND CLASS CITIZEN

Armed only with my reputation a few selective overtures I venture to make
Positive responses from the other party I'd be happy to take
Rigid replies with no signs of humor the only forthcoming sound
Seems once again the object of my affection doesn't want me around.

Available ladies demand confidence from their guys to the most positive degree
Not found in pill form upon a drugstore shelf to rescue me
Withdrawing from the scene my head bowed down once again
Seemingly never destined to call a female person a friend.

"Why do they settle for others always telling me no?"
"Is the option of continuous mental health therapy the only way to go?"
Words of endearment so special; sweeter than honey
In the spiritual sense a warm feeling more important than money.

An Unwilling Socialite

Offering an evening on the town to an ungrateful lass
Thinking she was better than me a member of the upper class
Like a good soldier the frigid journey did she make
Not impressed by the positive atmosphere I tried to create.

A second journey created the presence of instant replay inside her mind
Happy to see her home though worried parents she came to find
A minor sewing repair requested of her at the end of the day
When it was over a threesome had many angry words to convey.

A final connection upon the day of the super bowl game
Gave the unified family many opportunities to put me to shame
A future doctor was destined to become the love of her life
For me a consolation prize, a final exit without pageantry or strife.

A New Circle

Renewing a friendship via a visit to a bagel pub
Introduced to three seniors offering a reservoir filled with additional love
Common topic conversation made the relationship seem created a long time ago
Feelings of acceptance so promising in this "Nice to meet you" show,

My physical appearance and weight loss gave this assembly additional appeal
The pain I felt too in a father's lament over his son's weight problem so real
Talking about social memories at a time well in the past
Explaining together that tokens of unhappiness in the mind not intended to last.

Everyone's agenda so predictable yet subject to change
Around the meeting at the pub everything else must be rearranged
Future encounters welcomed by all having a voice
Opportunities to connect with well meaning people a positive choice.

Testimony Of The Gossip Brigade

Sinful words of condemnation upon the tongues of a privileged few
Strong messages of social expertise upon the social upstart fall anew
Office policies will quickly end your hopes for social assendency
Replaced instead by increasing waves of doubt and regular visits to medical psychiatry.

Air pollution a common trait in quest of female mind control
Whispered secrets of male demise stimulate the female social soul
A time to move forward; a time to retreat
A time to forget; a time to compete.

Ongoing hostility coupled with lies
The end of the road for a minor league type of guy
In over his head with the brigade players you see
Burying him forever through their dark visions of social mastery.

One Of Many Roads To Choose

Twenty four hour trials of character that never seem to end
Rubbing elbows with those today tomorrow no longer called a friend
Navigating slowly through a modern day minefield under a cloud of despair
Continuously searching my inner soul for a trace of fortitude somewhere.

The realm of intrigue continuously casting righteous expectations aside
An inner light of iron amid a sea of darkness my only positive guide
Accept the pain, accept the blame the newest martyr you can be
Another fallen corpse in the modern era of social chivalry.

A backbone of steel from your numerous foes never thought of upon their deception plate
Connecting with the chief executioner in the near future a festive date
An opportunity to hope for mercy; an opportunity to strike a blow
Only a hidden voice come judgement day tells me where to go.

Resolutions For A New Year

For a trimmer waistline to extra calories I bid an affectionate farewell
In terms of diet programs now under your spell
A habit of constant yawning must come to an end
Additional hours of rest now a national health trend.

Learning to speak properly though mouth wash is near
Looking through the contents of a dictionary to impress those I hold most dear
Bonding with relatives for whom I've had little time before
No one knows what the future for us holds in store.

Exhibiting more kindness to the weak and the small
Prior to running and walking with distinction I must learn how to crawl
Free time for volunteer hours for worthy tasks now at hand
Only by pushing aside materialism can we collectively enrich our great land.

Permanently Tied To The Cradle

After two decades blowing out the candles confidently on my own
Thinking I could make crucial decisions setting my special personal tone
Illness overtook me; left me lying flat on my back
In handling life's crisis moments not yet ready to learn the proper knack.

Placed upon a special diet I gradually shrunk in size
The former overweight underachiever now deemed a worthy prize
Everyday so cautioned; "Are you wearing your hat?"
"A future date with pneumonia the level you're playing at."

Food portions once so large now so small in view
Regular restaurant locations through the front door entrance no longer remembering you
A silent state of rebellion so immature the way things are
Turned around by the hands of fate a good trip for you so far.

The Real Woman Behind The Mask

Posing for a place upon Mount Rushmore when I approached you the cashier
The state of your well being to your customers not exactly clear
A trace of your accent when you spoke; probably a new resident from a foreign land
A temporary position in this food entity the initial step in your future to command.

A beloved husband in your life to assist you along the way
A bitter divorce battle involving broken promises your former other half now always to pay
Memories of unspoken hardship in a continuing battle ridden undeclared war
Even now temporarily affected by sounds of gun fire outside your front door.

Laboring with dedication for small wages as the boss tells you what to do
Coming in under the weather with no benefits with a case of the flu
Listening with one ear to the silly words of old men trying to proposition me
Maybe a mask covers my face to guarantee eight continuous working hours of stability.

Digging Deep Inside My Wallet

Graciously assisting my kids in the world of music an extra curricular happy zone
Claiming membership in the only world to call their very own
Confidently approaching parents, legal guardians, and next of kin
On my own a challenge of the greatest magnitude I just cannot win.

Displaying smiles, armed with words of endearment I appeal to their inner pride
Unwilling to part with personal attachment; few are willing to take my side
Surrounded by signs of resignation, I look to the heavens for guidance to be
Torn between conflicting emotions once again I borrow from my personal treasury.

My adopted children are covered, their biological connections just evaporate away
Another monetary crisis is over; again the guardian uncle has had to pay
Some day in the form of a resolution I'll sing another song
Despite what the parents and the school board thinks; in the eyes of the children I can do no wrong.

No Stamps Available Today

The movement of envelopes through a circulation process to be
The continuing raising of rates creating a climate of urgency
Racing to the local sales area to beat a proposed deadline
Their supplies non existent to my sorrow I find.

Off to another source I arrive ahead of time
Told to cool off my anxieties before I graciously claim what is mine
Saved from another voyage in the rain so grey and so bleak
The contents of my envelopes so time consuming and unique.

Slowly with measured steps through puddles to the delivery site I go
In search of a finished product to a company I must show
Only twenty two hours of waiting till the next phase of the process takes place
An opportunity to chase stardom or to fall flat on my face.

Through A Windshield

Cruising slowly through a main artery as part of a traffic jam
A large stone like receptacle descended causing us to shiver like a lamb
Glass debris covered the occupants of the front row seat
Escaping only with unsettled nerves was certainly no small feat.

Riding alone on the chosen path to the occupational center
A holiday season was upcoming; one for the family to certainly remember
Suddenly a turkey bounced off the ground giving me an excuse to cry
Through the pain and the tears my mouth continuously forming the word "Why?"

Friends close to the dashboard seat belts dangling innocently at their side
Not interested in practicing safety to severely damage their existing macho pride
A reason to stop in front of us anxiously applying the brake
A bloody picture of pain exchanged for a few moments of prevention not willing to take.

A Lack Of Caution On The Main Drag

Following my usual ritual in the direction of home around the hour of five
A disabled delivery vehicle in my path an escape route ready to contrive
Suddenly crossing a second lane in the direction of the center island near by
The vehicle to my left ready to react or ready to die.

Putting on his brakes the vehicle moved slowly in a spin to the left side
The company letters of the delivery vehicle witnessed up close with a sigh of relief rather than
shallow pride
An early accident of the new year avoided as if anyone cared
A witness at the right location my luck just to be there.

Having to happen so soon after the season of St. Nick
An abnormal act taken by a driver not at the top of his game perhaps even sick
Dodging another bullet as I journeyed silently down the road
Just to be alive more valuable to me than the largest pot of gold.

Working Both Sides Of The Street

Hanging a left into the driveway of my working pad
Watching out for a dump truck whose odor leaves my morning breath sad
One hundred yards later or so I enter through the back door
Past men in blue talking about their families and last night's baseball score.

In the courtroom judicial wisdom attempts to administer fairness to all
Sometimes in domestic cases it's really a tough call
Remembering those days now gone by as I take my seat
Remembering the issues involved in the office located across the street.

There a lonely old man opened the door for me
Fighting a losing battle against the disappearance of chivalry
Awaiting the traffic pilgrims from many locations with tickets to pay
In another courtroom a judge allowed them a verbal statement to say.

Outside, motorists feed the meters like little animals at the local zoo
Penalties are given out as protection for law abiding citizens like me and you
Tickets are written as a squad car's horn goes off again
Our system at times so flexible at times unwilling to bend.

So Important Today: No Room For Sentimental Reasons Tomorrow

Cutting out a newspaper clipping for information today
Soon inside a scrapbook page its contents will lay
Tapeing a sitcom showing the problems of suburbanites all on display
Years later inside an old box dust particles on its surface do play.

Keeping everything a motto I carried through the years
Parting with anything I keep fighting back my tears
Unable to clean the floor for its surface I never do see
From the day of my birth till now a genuine cardboard dynasty.

When cleaning day comes I move many things around
The trash can remains empty as those around me frown
Good organization something in the future to try on for size
Saying goodbye will win me open space as the number one prize.

My Hair: Stimulating Changes For My Adoring Public

My physical presence offers many inviting attributes to the naked eye
That makes many types of suitors want to say hello instead of goodbye
Above my intellect I want everyone to see the top of my head
Working myself into a frenzy in front of a mirror each night before I go to bed.

Starting with curls I created lasting excitement for a two week span
That had appreciative trackers doing double time in hope of calling themselves my new old
man
Taking on a regular style everyone's blood pressure came down a degree
Though many opportunists continued to voice approval when observing me.

Now my shaven head takes my feminine allure off center stage
Former admirers now shake their heads then move on to another page
Recharging my batteries at home I now get plenty of sleep
My boyish appearance in front of a mirror affords me continuing relief.

A New Boundary Of Inconvenience

Small steps and large steps taken upon a concrete plain
Now a sea of mud goes against the grain
Scepticism arrives again as the composition of creation deepens in mystery
Architects of sweat and toil making the move through an eye sore disguised as luxury.

Around the boundary people wander down a busy street
Dodging cars and construction rigs another day of life their personal treat
During the spirit of detour pedestrians manufacture personal groans
Soon replaced by squad cars amid the presence of orange cones.

Breathing in humidity flavored with concrete dust
Too many pressing thoughts for the majority to raise a fuss
The question always lingers; "Will this building campaign ever end?"
Where foes at the outset accept the final result as friends.

Retiree vs Trainee

Voicing the words goodbye and farewell for over a year
Tears of sentimentality never falling into my root beer
Over the course of many seasons I stood my ground
Now ever so willing to surrender the keys to the new kid in town.

Toward my words of wisdom little emotion has he shown
Turns out the independent soul has a few ideas of his very own
His centerpiece for action is a machine Apple by name
Keeping viruses away the master plan of his game.

The price of experience not everyone is willing to pay
His call for help will fall upon deaf ears over the course of one final cold Autumn day
When I was young all the right moves belonged to me
Now as the shadows lengthen I move slowly over the ashes of my own personal misery.

The Big Itch

Cooling off after another hot Summer day
Without thinking this time my appearance would pay
Feeling at this moment I was exceptionally clean
A coming out party for mosquitos exceptionally mean.

Soon I was scratching here, there, and everywhere
A possible cure in the medicine cabinet was not there to share
In desperation appealing to family pride
A special cure no longer willing to hide.

The bottle of magic lotion did not last long
Covering the battlefield like a hostility ending song
Falling asleep with the latest bites proudly on display
Unable to keep the smallest offensive creatures at bay.

The Inquisition

Inviting some friends after school to come visit me
Hoping later on to win a spot in their social fraternity
The homeowner decided to remain as part of the entertainment room
Several questions later my inner joy had turned to gloom.

To another office I ventured as a guest
Not thinking about all the sins I'd be called upon to confess
A look of suspicion as I began to feel surprisingl;y mad
Watching all the notes written down upon a legal pad.

A first date with a special someone not turning out as it was supposed to be
Our captives during wartime never faced such misery
Two life stories balanced awkwardly upon a single plate
Solitude never looked so good compared to this first date.

My Brother / My Headache

In a large family my achievements were top of the line
Others on the list a safety net hoping to find
I made my grades on and off the field keeping the ladies happy too
While those drowning upon the sea of unhappiness kept asking me what to do

Words were offered as I kept up my adventuresome pace
In the game of life always focused upon the race
Parents and siblings could only do so much
The sounds of frustration caused us to fall out of touch.

Perhaps a long step program to serve as a position guide
To get at the source of the pain hidden deep inside
The scars we carry some visable some not at all
In search of that elusive victory no matter how small.

Independent Drivers On Highway USA

The odd couple on the road keeping their speed at 35
Through illness and hardship happy to be alive
A long line of impatience forming to their rear
The highway sign says 65 to those who read it clear.

In need of gas ready to make a turn removed from the curb
In the middle to his left another motorist must swerve
A horn goes off as another car comes into the space
Time to make some noise as the "Who Me" vehicle disappears without a trace.

Into the flow will I go as someone prepares to turn
Halfway into the movement my stomach begins to churn
I assumed a turn that never was meant to be
Running into some stranger on another day of highway infamy.

Setting forth on a short trip the light to me reads red
Honking horns and passing cars make me wish I stayed in bed
Being safe behind the wheel I wish to remain on the road
Traffic rules for others so different and so bold.

Leader Of A Rock And Roll Band

Exposed to the sounds of the forefathers a baptism for the young
Playing their records over and over memorizing all the words they ever sung
Experimenting at an early age instead of following the regular academic ABC's
Determined some how in the future to bring the music world to its knees.

Adding some talent to create a new identity falling off the wall
Playing for publicity before local crowds never large often very small
Through the spirit of unification an agent came together with a hit song
In your fantasy world of honest legal creation nothing ever would go wrong.

The stamp of complete creativity you placed upon your head
After years of painful argumentative discussion you put your group's unity to bed
In the hour of your greatest accolade in response to a final show
The pain and suffering of years gone by in your heart never willing to let go.

Two Wheel Cadillac

I first noticed him shifting from side to side
Alone with his thoughts on a Sunday morning ride
Dressed up in his working clothes his age not a reason
To deny him the opportunity to travel during any touristic type accepted season.

The tires appeared worn often begging for air
As a substitute for gasoline his foot power always appeared to be there
How many miles he traveled stored up safely inside his head
Contact with modern day motorists the only thing he seemed to dread.

After he passed me I turned off the great divide
Willing to pay big dollars to continue my daily transportation ride
His left foot then his right foot kept him moving along
As a member of the common sense travel group to which he belonged.

TEN AT THE TABLE

Arriving separately in groups of twos and threes everyone claims ownership to a chair
A time for small talk on recent memories a good reason to be there
The waitress arrives with menus like blankets folded over her arms
In a matter of seconds patience becomes her greatest charm.

Transmitting the verbal orders to a small pad in her hand
Trained a long time ago to handle one patron alone or large numbers of a hungry band
Now the journey to the kitchen eventually to fill every plate
In the minds of the hungry; "How much longer must we wait?"

Checking upon the needs of others then to the large multitude a second return
Hoping everything is in order that no one's personal happiness has taken a wrong turn
With a smile at the end of the meal the checks are placed upon the table
Now ready to depart members of a local working crew so contented and so stable.

IN PURSUIT OF NUTRITIONAL ENRICHMENT

An early morning hour the day has just begun
Waiting patiently for a door to open ready to have some fun
Assigned to a booth I've resided in many times before
Looking at the selections when a decision is made I have to look some more.

Starting with some coffee watching patiently as other patrons file in
Over the road travelers or carbon copy locals wondering where to begin
Cleaning off my plate acting out my morning dream
No breakfast spots upon my shirt for once I've kept it clean.

Check in hand I leave a tip and journey across the floor
Upon payment for my latest feast I glide right out the door
Satisfaction is written on my face as I settle in for the long drive home
Eating well is a luxury whenever part of a group or dining out alone.

PRIVATE CELEBRATION

Another year has passed the calendar seems to say
On the issue of celebration you would not have it any other way
A great big cake with many candles on top
When your guests began arriving the sound of the doorbell never seemed to stop.

At your major base of operations the guests wait in vain
Thinking you encountered car trouble or simply missed your train
Party hats and decorations never to be used
In the spirit of the moment many honestly felt cheated and abused.

Tomorrow with a hop and a skip again you will arrive here
Singing happy birthday to yourself grinning from ear to ear
For us another ordinary day as we watch the hands on the clock
Silently in our minds remembering the celebrations we can count on and those we cannot.

TOO MANY POTS ON THE STOVE

Traveling in political circles amid back room diplomacy where everything's at
In the center of creation upon his back a loving pat
Projects often started never finished at the end
For this character trait other available parties always willing to condemn.

Appointments followed by conversation the telephone ringing off the hook
On the subject of control and manipulation remember always he wrote the book
Concerning loyalty always willing to bring forth extra rope
Looking openly for new alliances upon his shoulders alone unable to cope.

Advising others on life's greatest mysteries always how to work things out
Despite non passing test scores always displaying great personal clout
Personal issues coming forth not intended for innocent ears
Do your job in silence or future retaliation will justify all your fears.

Wanting only to do my job never questioning his right to the throne
In the dark on procedures relegated to the sub intelligent zone
Time passes on as he continues his journey along the patronage trail
The loyalties of those closest to him never to rise never to sail.

An Office Sandwich

Coming in out of the cold to a reception so sunny
One liners coming forth so fast making the end result seem just as funny
Not a coffee house or a protest march however united as one
Posters on the wall demonstrating anything possible could be done.

Seconds become minutes as a heavy lethal dose of magnetism took hold
Through the offerings of an entertainer and a charmer always promising always bold
Over in the corner sat the extra in a two piece band
His mode of service not fashionable in the local community's political land.

Asking for assistance to improve day by day
Under the microscope his type of services would turn blue skies grey
Through active participation asked to give up a life of his own
Navigating a straight arrow existence in an otherwise free enterprise zone.

Never Enough Room In The Car

For the trip plans of preparation already set
Curtailment of newspaper and mail delivery already met
Behind the wheel the driver ready and eager to pull away from home
Looking unsuccessfully for his driver's license miles later in a nonspeeding zone.

Working feverishly to pack the camping equipment upon the roof
Too many non essentials if you really want to know the truth
The homemaker of the family full of confidence saying "I know the way"
The road map for the trip left on the living room table for use another day.

As a teenager the young man his cousin wanting to impress
Showing off his interest his own personal recreational success
Miles into the journey searching the crowded spaces within the back seat
His favorite video the guardian of solitude back home in company does keep.

A little angel campaigning for a puppy for such a long time
Promising in a solemn sense of honesty to take care of what's mine
Food, water, and pictures of the new addition to relatives ready to show
A few blocks away the sounds of lonliness from a pet when someone lets go.

A Pilgrimage to City Hall

Through the passage of raindrops amid the mud of construction toil
An awkward arrival upon the steps of political soil
Through a tunnel to a place of patience in a reception line
Through a weapons screening device the weapons of intrigue hidden just fine.

To the second floor another line waiting for me
Asked to return due to the absence of proper ID
Soon upon a bench thoughts of indecision crossed my mind
A sudden source of inspiration for me a successful find.

Back to the first floor to pay my dues
Up again to the office of documents a stroke of good fortune mine to use
Receiving my copies so happy to get this out of the way
Told by a hard working clerk to have a good day.

Somewhere Between Lost and Found

A long period of effort to bring my formal education to a close
Soon proudly wearing a cap and gown to cover my party clothes
Leaving my paper in the yellow vehicle resting on the back seat
Without its presence in the Dean's Office my degree requirements unable to complete.

Dropping a special ring which opened all the doors during my travels
The loss of this ring temporarily caused my life to stop and unravel
Hoping for a messenger of mercy to discover my loss and turn in the prize
Turning my period of anxiety into a period of learning from foolish to wise.

Bringing my child for some toys and food to the mall
A turn of my head and he wasn't there anymore at all
After notifying security a continuing period of anguish began
Young ones no longer safe at the local playland.

Not Really Looking Your Age

Physical fitness a daily pattern on which I run
Beads of perspiration along with heavy breathing my idea of fun
No alliance with calories or inertia do I claim to make
A healthy appearance an award I want to take.

Continuously reading as I acquire wisdom for the ages
Increasing my intellectual capacity as I turn the pages
Information available for my ears through conversations of those older than me
Avoiding mistakes made by others a centerpiece of my philosophy.

Pushing yourself as part of a daily routine
Not having regrets later on when on a life support machine
Some in the absence of years leave their mark
Others in the mold of senior type status never really make a start.

A Family Divided

The Patriarch on the subject of conflict always defending the flag
Dissent against the spirit of democracy always leaving him sad
The remaining family united on the issue against going to war
Leaving the fighting to others at our Nation's front door.

Major sports idolatry never finds us as comrades in arms
Never confessing to the other sides star athlete's numerous charms
Some of us glow in the celebration of victory at a hot spot in town
The rest drown in the sorrows of their personal misery with no consoling kinship around.

One look at my current beau was all my dad could take
Cautioning me later against making a major mistake
Heartfelt emotions would continue to affect my soul
Not allowing words of wisdom to infiltrate and take control.

A promotion for one a penalty for the rest
The next move for the majority anyone's guess
Farewell to my friends with memories soon melting into a historical past
In the quest for material advancement sadly good times are not allowed to last.

UNCHARTED WATERS

Last year in the late innings many games given away
During the off season the general manager would have his say
Paying big money a new star was welcomed into town
In the spirit of victory the voices of doom never offered forth an opposing sound.

Coming in to pitch whenever the game was on the line
Despite some moments of uncertainty, success to the locals was very kind
In the biggest series the manager threw caution to the wind
In the process commiting a destructive psychological sin.

Victory was in the making till the plate disappeared that fateful day
The monarchs of the diamond ambushed the locals on the field of play
When the smoke had cleared the Amazings' were not amazing anymore
Many would second guess the action taken as they swallowed the final score.

SAYING GOODBYE TO VICTORY

After a championship season that put a curse to rest
Among the available free agents certainly one of the very best
Hearing convincing words of persuasion signing his name on the dotted line
Continuing along the road to Cooperstown a journey so very fine.

As the innings have mounted a hundred pitches to his name
Counting on the bullpen to preserve a victory just the same
When the bullpen has faltered a painful experience to beare
Playoff hopes of the locals on the brink of ruin so unjust and so unfair.

A rotation on shakey ground when the ace no longer can go nine
In the minors or on other team rosters a solution hoping to find
A round table representation of the club's executive bigs
Inside this collective bag of resourcefulness the powers that be must dig.

Four Legged Expectations

Round and round the horse traveled at a high rate of speed
In the future millions in prize money his principal deed
The winner's circle to claim perhaps even the Triple Crown
Nothing it seems possible would ever bring him down.

Able to overcome every barrier when put to the test
Finishing first always seemed to put the objections of critics to rest
At Churchill Downs running away from the rest of the field
His principal rivals in defeat ready to concede ready to yield.

At Baltimore the ugly hand of fate reared up its ugly head
The one tragedy that all investing owners always dread
In the beginning a race forward for success in the zone
In a moment a career ended due to multiple fractures of a hind leg bone.

Comparing Notes

Accepting another invitation to the building along the road
Marching wearily along the path where the combination of interstates and clouds of dirt
unfold
Something to do with food and awards for a chosen few
Warm bodies are required today as empty seats just will not do.

After a greasy breakfast a cup of coffee in my hand
A familiar stranger notices me as we begin a verbal jam
Our conversation centers around clients, office structure, plus personalities too
Management at times good otherwise still figuring out what we have to do.

The centuries old issue of quality vs quantity once again rears its ugly head
Like a three headed monster in a space built for two never intended to put to bed
Shrugging our collective shoulders as the notes of the same old song
Never allow us an easy exit only the opportunity to play along.

ONE BIG ROOT

The undergrowth around the house big enough to relate to the Amazon
Garden tools coupled with human sweat an alliance ready to try on
The elderly leader pointing out where and when to launch the attack
Once completed, a sense of accomplishment, never having to look back.

One big underground entity refused to surrender with out a fight
Witnessing the meekness of the ivy and tree limbs to him a negative sight
"Within the ground I'm connected"; "Within the ground I'll stay"
"Something greater than your total power is needed to move me this sunny afternoon day".

The elderly leader rolled up her sleeves and began to pull
Bent in half like a horseshoe her power determined to triumph before the first snows of the yule
The underground entity resisted with all the strength at his command
After a few minutes that seemed forever permanent separation triumphed over permanent
connection to the land.

UNDER THE COVER OF DARKNESS

On numerous issues management and the union could not agree
For seven million commuters a holiday gift a local calamity
A trip to school, a trip to work, or just moving around
On the question of inconvenience seven million souls voiced their collective sounds.

Standing in line or negotiating a ride
The locals could not hide their emotions inside
Businesses in true holiday spirit were forced to close down
While politicians through local interviews reminded stranded commuters they were still around.

Across the bridge they traveled at the crack of dawn
Held hostage on the issue of respect the populace labeled themselves "Holiday Pawns"
After a long day with no settlement in sight
Across the bridge marched a sea of humanity into the cold Winter's night.

Financial Connection With Ecuador

Sitting upon a stool behind the window she appeared so buoyant and tall
In reality when the vault was closed in person so focused and small
Always offering forth a company lingo to the next customer in line
Receiving the same statement from those short of cash that everything was fine.

Disappearing for a couple of weeks on a vacation trip she wanted to take
I caught up with her in the parking lot carrying a birthday cake
She approved of my humble request to call her by her first name
Without hesitation I would have remained formal without incurring any blame.

Always on schedule I try to be the first in line
To hear her promise to watch over my money so professional and kind
As workaholics our days always seem to run together
Years of toil upon our tombstones the only thing about us the world will remember.

It's Only Words

Behind a desk looking her directly in the eye
Factual information offered forth symbolizing the old college try
Utilizing bold strokes the arbitrator attempted writing everything down
A silent system of filtration in place operating conveniently without a sound.

Lukewarm assurances given that in the final analysis integrity would prevail
A few months later the office building holding on to her unopened mail
A new communicator appeared as both sides traveled back to square number one
Altered evidence gave artificial credibility to the misdemeanors that were done.

Soon in the near future a visit to the structure representing all
To sit in humble silence awaiting a tainted judgement call
In the continuing gender conflict victims will involuntarily always appear
Fairness always found on paper in reality never on a higher level to be held dear.

A Cleansing Of The Mind

A rainy Monday brought forth a constant state of gloom
As three smooth operators gathered together in a secluded recreation room
Talking quietly about an issue lingering on through the years
A solemn rite of understanding washed down through many tears.

The elements of kindness thought vinegar could be changed to maple syrup some way
The boldness of his effort for the surrounding audience sadly a heartbreaking visual display
No amount of sweetness could successfully penetrate the sour hostile form
Denying herself a re-entry ticket; another opportunity to be reborn.

The apostles told their kind cousin, "Independent you should be"
Better to chart a new course of work time isolation than share in group style misery
Save your health and your charms for hours you call your very own
Allow your reputation to develop and grow among your friends like others you have already known.

Blue Star Fire Extravaganza

Heavy clouds of emerging smoke covering the main artery in town
Gridlock conditions created so no one individual quickly can get around
An early afternoon appointment where friends and relatives gather for the last time
Police officers waving their hands franticly supporting traffic control by design.

Patience called upon as the temperature arrow moves into the tropic zone
A fifty five year friendship recipient repeating prayers sitting quite alone
Arriving home another legal notice conveniently dropped upon my plate
In the spirit of fond memories some financial renumeration actions will just have to wait.

Thanks to gridlock city the usual route is tabled on behalf of Plan B
No additional stress is created with daylight available to see
The next of kin now mature showing off a new generation they call their very own
Upon a DVD loving images of one who made it possible continuously being shone.

Tomorrows first edition a report on the mischief causing it all
Daily plans of life often come to a halt or temporarily stall
Anxiety and concern develop when deadlines are not met
For a loving mother at this time the sun had already set.

DRYNESS MULTIPLIED

The old cooler along with the empties disappeared out into the night
Dry mouths took turns repeating words that the situation was unfairly not right
Messengers rode off in search of additional supplies
Medications and problems of thirst remained an inconvenience in the sets of tired eyes.

The hierarchy once again was playing games
A new administration warned us that things would not be the same
Stand in line at the fountain so happy to wait
Additional money out of your wallet for water I promise to take.

Bring your own from home or try consuming gasoline
The thought of that in your stomach always so mean
As the problem continues everyone shakes their head
Political intrigue maintains total control never to rest or be put to bed.

ADDRESSING THE CORE OF A PROBLEM

Observing a situation where total effort is on display
The wrong solution allows the architect of participation toward the wrongful piper the price to pay
Meeting in secret when the professional is home on leave
The representative of improved office morale came away empty handed on this issue I believe.

Three times the normal load of paperwork placed in his hands
More early morning hours necessary to cover the ritual as only he can
Calling up the connection to see what went wrong
Another example of egomania pushing forward the wrong unity song.

Everyone knows the location of the exit sign
A future one way trip in the dreams of all at the end of the line
The hands of time passing slowly, too slowly with the illogical patterns hanging over our work site
Political connection never the right choice to make wrong agendas right.

On The Ropes

Facing painful images every day on the TV screen
With no end in sight part of a nightmarish like continuing dream
Wondering outloud sometimes how my son is doing in this long lasting war
The shock of seeing an officer in uniform advancing toward my front door.

My little girl became ill soon after reaching the age of three
Many visits to specialists trying to find an answer to this deepening mystery
With no improvement every family member now knows the score
My beloved youngest born destined never to see the age of four.

Many years of effort I offered forth on the assembly line
Collected dirt under my fingernails which suited me just fine
Promised more money along with benefits by the people at the top
Concealing a hidden secret that my association with the company would soon have to stop.

Behind in my mortgage payments due to a disease called bad luck
Cruising along at the top of my game till lightning struck
Now my emotions find me far removed from my peak
Soon to be living like a gypsy out on the street.

An Extra Dose Of Relaxation

Caught up in my dreams catching up on my rest
My customers always refer to me as one of the best
So blissful my thoughts as time slowly slips away
Looking at the clock my boss wonders how often I plan to behave this way.

My following anxiously searching the front entrance through feelings of hope
Silently praying that a faulty alarm clock is the problem in scope
Soon after I wander in a sheepish grin upon my face
I'm just a working girl not really married to this place.

In my absence the bread would go stale along with the muffins inside of the boxes
The patrons meanwhile would silently stare at the TV in search of news reporting foxes
The milk would turn sour and my boss would become dizzy
Ready to call it a day and drive home in his super charged lizzy.

6 AM - 10 PM

Awakening with a yawn to face the challenges of another day
Saying hello to the kitchen another breakfast on the way
Into the attic personal items to move around
Giving away your location as tired feet continue making sounds.

Back on the ground floor dirty rugs catch your gaze
The vaccum cleaner springs to life earning you future praise
Putting footwear slowly upon your wrinkled feet
Time to move the garbage out into the street.

Upon the couch you rest yourself through the reward of a well earned nap
The pace of early rising upon your energies constant labors often sap
Later with its arrow upon empty your stomach tells you so
Back into the kitchen to prepare another meal you must go.

Watching news shows on TV a bitter pill of negativity to take
Time to write some letters while I am still awake
Have to let my friends know I am still alive
A determined old girl full of vigor at the youthful age of 85.

SUCCESSFUL PEOPLE

Absenteeism his main contribution to a school system so unfair
Ignoring the voices of authority with hardly a care
One day an outsider told him in the future you would have to pay
By reversing directions on the stage with his classmates come graduation day.

Heaping scorn upon the minority who came unexpectedly into his life
From a distant land filled with poverty, disease, and war related strife
Differences understood slowly as a bonding of the minds came to be
Now a mutual package of respect endures where once reigned continuing hostility.

Forced to accept the burden of the young once daddy took a one way ride
The tears she shed could not control the hurt she felt inside
Job training offered her and her clan a new time honored lease
Now time offers her new challenges coupled with an inner sense of peace.

Wild and reckless until they closed the bars behind you one day
For abusing your rights in society a young man would have to pay
Years of counseling and meditation slowly brought you around
Now inside a machine shop a new trainee eager to learn can be found.

MEASURABLE PRECIPITATION

Small sized measures of hope fall upon the parched dry land
Saving a cash crop of a farm family instead of turning their acreage into sand
Enduring endless hours of toil from morning till night
Witnessing the fruits of their labor with all segments covered a wonderful sight.

Under the cover of plastic two boys gaze sadly across the field
The subject of their unhappiness; their team to the elements having to yield
Three months before responding favorably to this much anticipated recreational day
Now remorsefully resigned to a postponement or an unacceptable weather delay.

Under the slumbering eyes of local officials advanced warnings were not heeded
Rescue attempts for the victims slow in coming when much needed
Volumes of criticism were sounded with the seasonings of racial overtones
Many years in passing before the survivors completely removed from the danger zones.

MY RESIDENCY BEHIND A COUNTER

Everyday repeating a familiar journey to the coffee shop
A flow of patrons displaying individual examples of hunger that never seems to stop
I grab my pad and rush toward the field
In spite of rudeness and misunderstandings my smile never meaning to yield.

Patiently taking their orders always wanting to have it their way
My attention frozen in time for them from Monday through Saturday
Painstakenly repeating all directives for my pad to make them all secure
My humble figure upon local stargazers just exemplifying simple allure.

Washing dishes, running to the cash register, then picking up the phone
Too many people to answer to, never given quality time to ever be left alone
Aside from the men in uniform hearing about local favorites falling sick on any given day
Enthusiastically coming in all the time for I too have bills to pay.

America, America a land of opportunity though the streets were never paved with gold
I never accepted that theory though many times I've been told
Every work day another challenge I grab my bat and take a swing
From where I started out my daily routine now in this great land is everything.

RELOCATION

Twenty years of healthy living suddenly coming to an end
On the issue of family ties never considered a friend
Given an ultimatum thirty days to pack up and get out
On the legality of it all I could not complain, protest, or even shout.

The dog days of mid summer July heat shined down upon me
Destined on a continuing basis to separate calories you see
Desperately laboring to meet the deadline set down upon your paper
Heavily breathing in the humid like conditions like a rocket connected vapor.

The landlord in her negligence nailed me in small claims to a wall
Extracting money from me under her code of justice was quite a ball
Limping away from the battlefield for me a personal celebration
A small price to pay in quest of permanent separation.

MICHAEL MORPHINE

Six hours upon my stretcher in the E.R. I did keep
Desperately needing a friend to allow me the opportunity to sleep
Once safely entrusted to some temporary rest inside my hospital room
I called upon the local nurse to bring me Michael to temporarily remove my discomfort and gloom.

A few hours with Michael the relationship was complete
Amid my dryness and agony a sense of temporary relief
When Michael went on vacation the temporary symptoms returned again
To the nurse I gave an order; "Please find Michael", to me now an old friend

Once my surgery was completed to Michael an awkward goodbye
A constant source of reliability all together a really good guy
Now removed from the hospital setting a return to day to day living to be
I'll always remember my friend Michael in my hour of maximum need so dependable for me.

A FUTILE EFFORT TO SECURE PARENTAL APPROVAL

Falling in love amid feelings of joy, happiness, and anticipation
Praying that all those around me will accept her without reservation
Not wanting to spend the rest of my life alone
Not willing to accept token hostility during the coordination trip back home.

After the ringing of the door bell
A mother's anguish cast her under a hostility spell
Racing away from our twosome of mutual satisfaction
In a side room eagerly setting up a base camp of negative reaction.

Meanwhile Dad wearing a look of contentment gave my chosen one a hug
Motioning her to sit down after navigating across our fifteen year old rug
A sign of welcome well hidden within a prevailing environment of gloom
Tears started forming in the eyes of my beloved due to mixed feelings present within the room.

Her education was exceptional, her personality full of warmth and understanding
On issues regarding our future partnership; often compromising not very demanding
Acceptance into our family one challenge my sweetheart could never hope to win
Upon the day of her birth denied entry into our future because of the color of her skin.

SITTING ON A BAR STOOL

Occupying my usual position with potato chips and pretzels my friends tonight
Turning off the outside world as if someone cares about my plight
The regular bartender stops by eager to fill up my tank
Hearing voices discussing politics and women my hopes for a quiet evening quickly sank.

Nodding my head in agreement I pacify one then the other
A non voter and three time divorcee banging heads with me as their adoptive brother
On each issue information moves me to the head of the class
Anxiously looking for the bartender to once again fill up my glass.

Four hours later time again to go home
Removed from the hostilities in search of a quiet zone
At the front door my other half greets me with her complaining trend
Soon I'll be ready to go searching for my bar stool once again.

Tomorrow Is Here

Wisdom from the elders is passed out to all
Youthful ears capture the meanings when given the call
Preparation for the future on your plate on any given day
Never able to gain additional time from a magical era called yesterday.

The desire to excel depends upon the hunger in your heart
Controlling your future places you in a category called minority upstart
Isolation moves closer becoming your only friend
Voices of the majority make you hesitate never meaning to bend.

Education, employment, every day living, and love
Some endings end happily; others seem rough
A hidden voice may smooth out the rough images of pain
Only you alone can measure the magnitude of your own personal gain.

Floating Through The Golden Arches

In the darkness navigating quickly to be on time
A round trip ticket to be purchased for a regular commuting line
At the point of entry facing the prospect of more darkness on the inside
The hands of a clock moving too slowly to rescue my injured pride.

Depending cautiously upon a pepsi shapped machine to rescue me
Instructed by a street hustler in exchange for an assistance fee
Soon aboard the iron horse with a morning daily as my entertainment guide
Rows of houses, factories, and trees in the darkness decorating the countryside.

Moving slowly through the rain remembering the one who caused this pain
On time for continuing instructions as the innocent recipient of all the blame
Seeing the yellow lights ahead welcoming the hungry one and all
Time to fill up the stomach once again before hearing a repetitive proper behavior call.

Under A Sea Of paper

In search of order a cleansing process was begun
The creator of the mess; "Yes"; "I was the one"
Stuffing and dumping trying to close a heavy drawer shut
The only result of my effort a painful paper cut.

Wanting to discard at the same time wanting to save
In the back of my mind it's simplicity and structure that I crave
The stranger seated in front of me with contempt shaking his head
In silence offering me an unprofessional rating that I wanted to avoid instead.

Paper heavy when the yellow forms along the edges for all to see
Remnants of documents gathered from a recent century
Reminding myself constantly that this problem has to go
In control or totally confused the only options in this daily accessability show.

Come Next Monday I Am Going To

Start looking for the main road out of my town
Put less food on my plate extra calories no longer welcomed around
Create some forces to make my dreams come true
Dress up in my finest and start searching for a girl named you.

Be kind to my family to bind up old wounds
Be less envious over wedding announcements presenting new grooms
Control my frivolous spending with the future at hand
Spend some time at a local bar promoting my favorite band.

Start paying attention to some local civic affairs
Buy a repair kit and begin fixing up my old lawn chairs
The alarm suddenly rings at a quarter after three
A long night's slumber in dreamland has gotten the best of me.

Rain Delay

Survivors of the elimination tournament to meet in the championship game
A big moment in the life of an eleven year old too precious to tame
Family members gathered together down the first base line
If only the weather would cooperate we'd do just fine.

College rivals meeting at the end of a season some forty games long
Looked down upon by the experts they proved them all wrong
The issue of aluminum vs wood in the arsenal they swing
Major league scouts looking to sign some players taking in everything.

The lateness of the game on a late October Autumn night
With school on the agenda tomorrow sure to provoke a fight
The last championship for the home team some three generations ago
Memories in a young fan's mind through the raindrops continue to grow.

I Don't Know You / You Don't Know Me

Your phone ringing at an awkward moment of the day
A strange voice at the other end determined to have his say
Looking to speak with someone usually not available at this time
Calling back later the pleasure is all mine.

A look of bewilderment in seeking out your identity
Despite your longevity on the job still a complete mystery to me
No services have you dropped recently into my lap
Two separate entities coming to life after a life long non engaging nap.

In the future maybe you'll help us maybe you won't
As for an additional surprise phone contact kindly please don't
In private industry time is money while government sources continuously waste it away
Now through a desperate move for redemption your carelessness will have to pay.

Positive Thoughts About Better Tomorrows

In the afternoon out of the blue a sudden request
Put aside your work temporarily in favor of a recess
A special guest on high technology will tell you what's in store
Another false promise of unity with major problems on the agenda no more.

The hierarchy is promoting self service as a major boom
New workers added to the payroll will eliminate your temporary gloom
Calls on the issues everyone will still have to take
Promises based on superficial information everyone will still have to make.

Success stories will develop if only the systems combine
A continuing dream of everyone under one roof still hoping to find
The cost of the program the budget committee willing to pay
Taking the funds out of another program somewhere along the way.

Nucleus Of A Relationship

Sounds of wisdom from your lips capturing my gaze
Cheerful notes of opportunity from an intellectual lost in the maze
Accepting the fact I have miles to travel as I continue to grow
Together in the proper setting the seeds of our relationship we continue to sow.

Words of praise as I finish a task
Tender moments of understanding directed toward me without having to ask
Prior to your arrival thinking about a new start
Over a short period of time you've captured my heart.

Our agenda upon the table never too big never too small
Thinking about each other never allowing divided feelings to set up a wall
The passion of the time captured through the unification of our souls
Eager to continue the pursuit of mutual happiness in our established roles.

INJURED BY ANOTHER POISONED ARROW OF INDIFFERENCE

In quest of success walking a fine line
Acknowledging others not enough respect for them I find
Practicing individualism instead of becoming a centerpiece of the crowd
Future considerations for my peace of mind wrapped up in a shroud.

Upsetting the apple cart with a minute provocation
My form of idealistic behavior encouraged to take a long term vacation
A mode of completion followed day to day along the dock
Destined for removal as the wrong kid on the block.

No support from the top, tears alone offered forth at home
A wrong turn along the way landing me in the Twilight Zone
Time alone the pill of success far removed from the mind
Emotional wounds of fate securely in the future will I bind.

FOOTPRINTS IN THE SAND

Small steps dropping me off at various locations of food domain
About my expanding waistline at this time I will not complain
Games of chance coupled with amusement rides too
In the whole scheme of things many choices awaiting you.

Mountains of creativity available near the shore
A trip back to medieval times along with round table lore
Castles and kings mixed in with fair maidens and disease
Memories of epic battles bringing new subjects down upon their knees.

Teams of two hitting a ball over the net
Giving up a lucrative career in search of competition with no regret
Winning the big points in search of money, trophies, and fame
My local supporters in hope of an autograph making their claim.

Big bodies, small bodies, and those in between
Like a piece of bread inside a toaster their objective serene
Color me a nice golden brown from head to toe
Hoping in the future a skin doctor I'll never know.

MALE DOMINATION

Staggering in to the local diner trying to beat the heat
My stomach in need of replenishment in order to compete
Sitting down a menu was still minutes away
Not one lovely lady stepped forth with a monologue to say.

The food was good, for a second cup of coffee the patron needed cream
Still hoping for positive customer service just an impossible dream
At the counter money in hand I respectfully paid my dues
Remembering in the future another restaurant I would choose.

Brothers of a family or job seekers playing a hunch
With no improvement in procedure the end of the free lunch
Moving slowly through their paces trying to find their roles
Like a group of wandering gypsies a gathering of lost souls.

IN SPITE OF MY GOOD INTENTIONS

A grab bag at Christmas time offered satisfaction to a few
Experts in their field of celebration knew just what to do
Outsiders played a different angle like a Christmas song
Only when the music stopped their selection turned out very wrong.

Playing an idea through proper channels to make my numbers rise
Completing all the necessary steps in the form of professional disguise
When the time came for others to pick up the torch and run
Someone created a story based upon lies and falsehoods to spoil all my fun.

Observing a young attractive lady we matched up well in size
Caught up in my innocence I wasn't very wise
A simple invitation was pushed back in my face
Now the State House won't permit me to go and visit the place.

INSTANT REPLAY

Words of the temporarily idle now focused upon the bottom line
A gold mine for government inertia on everyone's wish list hoping to find
This task assigned to everyone's reliable, steady, stable nominee
Eager to bring home the bacon after another chapter of budget crisis history.

A journey completed as many before
Into the humidity leaving the cool air behind a closed door
Upon arrival a phone call breaks up a normal day
The gods of instability have their say.

Back into the morning glare as patience comes under siege
Too much responsibility upon one's shoulders to bring him to his knees
A second success as tempers remain under control
Communication problems alone can tear at the fabric of an inner soul.

RECIPE FOR PAIN

Five steps of decendency where the brave always go
Focusing on issues of knowledge of which little they know
From the top of their private mountain going down in a heap
A sudden appointment with an ambulance reluctantly they keep.

Five steps of ascendancy sometimes reduced to four or perhaps even three
In their mind their footwear is the problem for the world to see
Down they go as their head meets glass
After a period of recuperation their embarrassment too shall pass

As the sentinel at the front gate I have a close view
Anxious moments at any time giving accidents their just due
Everyone in the middle though shaken miraculously still alive
Signing up for a numbers program on counting to five.

CONTINUING TRENDS FROM CHILDHOOD

Never affected by a cup in the morning to come alive
Continuing this practice as an adult every day I do strive
Bubbles and sugar in a bottle never meant for me
Still captured by Type II as part of my medical history.

Strong consumption is a theme over which I do not boost
Fitting in as a youngster failed to win me an acceptancy toast
Sweating for a team never expecting to lose
With the excess I now carry around still searching for clues

No late hours for me when the sun goes down
Still yawning continuously the next day with the regulars around
Words off the street so offensively clear
Knowledgeable reinforcement always possible with a dictionary always near.

PANIC ATTACK

A feeling of dependency sounded off on the second floor
Only an hour had passed, already I hungered for more
Grabbing my purse I flew down the stairs
Into the hot summer sun the sultry humid air.

Opening my purse I shifted everything to the left then to the right
In my mind this action constituted a winner take all endurance fight
A repetitive action yielded no positive results in this game
My system in need of a craving other than White Castle by name.

After a few more seconds the fight taken out of me
The futility of my cause already relegated to the well traveled pages of history
The middle aged soul nearby certainly not a romantic catch
In the spirit of total humility I bravely solicited a match.

Back in Business

As the elements of closure began to recede
The hope of opportunity the chief executive no longer will impede
Busloads of players pockets lined with available cash
Even though by evening hour their bank accounts may crash.

No longer entertaining thoughts of travel to yonder Connecticut Shore
When a dozen local establishments of chance hold open their doors
Bells signal the process of victory or defeat
Settle into a comfortable chair for the right to compete.

Later holding a vigil over the emotional connection of the daily game
A sense of repetition when every day begins the same
The locals in their world of expectation so glad you came
While the politicians in the halls of government through finger pointing place the blame.

The Longest Weekend

The usual projects spoken for and done
The challenging search for relaxation and fun
Flood waters off the Delaware have begun to recede
Meanwhile a debate develops in the halls of government for those in need.

Charges and countercharges separated rivals with a unique political mind
Placing their futures on the next election and the votes they hope to find
Red shirts arrived to watch the spectacle unfold
For the nearby ears of journalists their stories waiting to be told.

Back on the home front the weather too humid and too warm
Physical labor in bits and pieces allowing weariness to be born
With my activities of progress I have a future date
Patience becomes my steady companion as now all I can do is wait.

CAUGHT NAPPING

Eyes closed with uncertainty beneath an evening dark sky
Searching for assistance in quest of upward mobility with no time to buy
At the bottom of the steps welcoming myself to my temporary home
For a few hours of sleep in the name of survival now all alone.

In the middle of my dream suddenly the sound of a faraway cry
The sound of an adversary asking me to get up and move on by
Slowly I arise to give him a piece of my mind
In search of his vision of stability I am so blind.

Throwing out a dose of nastiness I add a few more
The system has all the weapons as I labor in confusion trying to score
Out of my temporary lodging I try to remain sane
The end result of my confrontation; "Who is really to blame?"

IN THIS CORNER

Humidity on the guest list made itself at home
The populace in a confined enclosure, no one freely able to wonder and roam
An individual with a laser like stare focused away
Setting off a fuse in another ready for combat rather than play.

Words were exchanged as the melting pot boiled over
Missiles on a collision course like a time long ago during the month of October
Suddenly a hero in uniform jumped into the middle
Advancing the cause of peace to no one playing second fiddle.

The ashes of hostility expired only after a short struggle
As spectators to an act of violence we remained on the bubble
No tears were shed by either adversary not even a sob
As the guardian of our safety once again completed a professional job.

FAMILY REUNION

Gathered together after the passage of many years
The gathering through the passage of time produced few emotional tears
Targets were selected, initial salvos fired to affect all the spirits within
Egos were broken down despite the similar identity of related family kin.

Painful moments from childhood were offered forth with a new hostile slant
Hoping for an apology from the receiver so falsely eager to recant
Peace commissioners were absent as retaliation seized the moment during the ride
A situation where all could unleash the bitter feelings harbored deep inside.

At journey's end casualties departed from a battle scene one by one
In the spirit of hostility all were satisfied their personal battles had been won
Retreating to treat their wounds to go their own separate ways
The pains of youth so harsh when exploited in their final adulthood days.

ANOTHER MISCALCULATION

Receiving an invite to my most prestigious activity of the season
So large in scope held for more than one reason
Directions on paper to keep a blind individual in line
On the day of closure sadly so difficult to fine.

The continuing search for a street sign that never was there
Bringing to mind past misfortunes of mine with which to compare
Round and round in circles I traveled on another humid unsympathetic day
The food and company missed never to become part of my social resume.

Prematurely home I voiced my frustration for a few minutes or more
As the dark side of my social history reinvented an old original verbal score
Settling in for an evening meal of frustration as though nothing was amiss
Resigned to the fact my name permanently removed from another guest list.

THE KING OF CONSUMPTION

School chums marveled at how I put it away
My appetite for them a key to a larger payday
The first contest held appropriately at the college dorm
Not really a contest not really part of the norm.

I started consuming and soon was up by three
My worthy opponent eager to award me my chosen destiny
An infinite hunger for me even the mustard and the bun
While he left most of his desires under a chair in good fun.

Some left that day with a profit others with a scorn
Not really believing that a new career had been born
Earning my money through other endeavors a word for the wise
My stomach too large for a healthy man of my acceptable size.

COVERING UP FOR THEIR SINS

Signed up for a program as an alternative to the journey of no return
Becoming a responsible person; "Does anyone really learn?"
A bag of debris deposited a leak upon the floor
The wrong solution to the problem as the bag follows me out the door.

The evidence available for all to see and to smell
A voice of reason supports an act of correction as time will tell
Suddenly a flotilla of mops and a bucket does appear
A solution to this problem miraculously near.

This volunteer army of outsiders cleans up the mess
Upon the altar of probability their laurels rest
Twenty four hours later; "Will the demons of instant replay play it again?"
Or will an ounce of responsibility begin a long term local trend.

Noise Inc.

Moments of relaxation suddenly taken away
A worker with a leafblower puts his machine on display
Garbage and dust moved quickly around
No longer your car the cleanest in town.

Brooms and shovels from an era gone by
Pay your admission at the local museum to reflect upon these artifacts and sigh
Now the process only offers injury to the ear drum
Grass cutters and landscapers turn up the volume to get the job done.

No welcome signs put out when these guys begin their task
The result of noise pollution too long does it last
When the job is over much to one's relief
Time for a second cup of coffee or an additional hour of sleep.

One Hundred Degrees And Climbing

Brother Humidity like a blanket covered our humble town
With reality settling in only emergency vehicles making a sound
Local citizens lined up to splash in the community pool
Citizenry pressing forward when the time expired for those in the water to be cool

Manhole covers exploded as residents in need of electrical power bid a temporary goodbye
Those in need moved into new locations or remained at home and cried
Business owners bid farewell to profits and let the mayor know
An investigation was promised allowing both sides their personal feelings to show.

Rain was promised but humidity was stubborn and would not go away
Additional sufferings were hidden through rate hikes sure to come our way
Global warming like a cheap tourist not ready to leave our side
Taking a few casualties with a firm resolve we fight to maintain our pride.

One Overheated ATM Machine

Waiting patiently for a patron to usher me aside
A long wait ahead for me my only value guide
Others enter and after pushing buttons silently depart
As the temperature rises courtesy of the corporate heart

Condensation forming on the glass due to the coolness on the other side
Sounds of Happy Birthday echo through the walls to further humble my personal pride
As the line forms a look of resignation a collective product found
Another wave of Happy Birthday on the cooler side abundantly rebounds.

Sharing my thoughts of misfortune with the teller I put her on the spot
Seems to her like a power struggle between haves and have nots
In a pensive mood she adopts a policy of wait and see
Attach yourself to the corporate world to win your share of cooling always available AC.

Gaining An Edge

Hidden behind the scoreboard out in deep center field
For the home team a secret fifth wheel
As the pitches move at various speeds toward home plate
Knowing ahead of time the batter with destiny has a date.

Gathering the ground crew together for the mission ahead
A highway of opportunity has to be put right to bed
Those in the running now reduced to a walk
After the game lamenting the scene in a post game interview talk.

Hitting over the fences once part of your dreams
A company has created for you an elaborate scheme
While cupcakes are noted for the cream filling inside
The pop in your bat will show that the purity of the game has died.

Once thin in stature never referred to as a superman on the field
A doctor has the tonic to make the critics yield
Fly balls to the warning track now go over the wall
A consistent diet of success will push Cooperstown to give you a call.

The High Price Of Inconvenience

Clouds of doom gathering overhead
Soon after a personal crisis is put to bed
The falling rain allows stationary objects an option to float
Along with my neighbors in the same boat.

Rising humidity brings me down to my knees
Opening the window at 3 AM in search of a breeze
The smell of spoiled food with nothing to eat
Accepted promises of local leaders unable to keep.

Raising my voice in search of compensation
A better place than the Big Apple perhaps a reservation
The "Mini Katrina" found our resources not there at all
Rising expenditures in the future bestowed on the big and the small.

A Majestic Vessel Of Commercial Enterprise

Safely anchored in the center isle never to float above the waves of any ocean
Professional employees of shirt and tie connection united in their devotion
A composition of home appliance tools for those of town and city
So far ahead in the art of salesmanship; for their rivals little profit at the risk of pity.

Waiting patiently as minutes pass by no salesperson at my side
In quest of an emergency purchase the locals have no pride
Through the passage of resignation advised to visit the others across the road
No enthusiasm for my presence; only indifference I am sold.

Welcomed by the captain as the newest member of the crew
Taking care of my request in the spirit of capitalistic colors true
Carrying on a conversation at a slow and friendly pace
Destined to leave with a sense of satisfaction a smile upon my face.

MY ADOPTED FINANCIER

On my first day no thoughts centered on a time frame 30 years down the road
Fast forward to the present a strange bill of goods I've been sold
Short of money a desperate move is made
The future of millions dependent upon a passing grade.

A stranger playing with my money capitalsm is his game
If he plays his cards right no one is to blame
However if he makes a wrong move the bottom of the basket falls to the floor
An uninvited guest named Poverty enters through my front door.

Another lane added to Main St; Wall St. is his name
When tax increases alone don't work times will never be the same
Pleasant thoughts on retirement soon to come to a stop
Laboring mightily at my cluttered desk till the moment that I drop.

FOLLOWING PAM

Never dreaming in a million years to be following thee
Brought together by chance as part of my morning hunger delivery
Thoughts centered upon pancakes, eggs, and all the right stuff
Suddenly concentrating on you as if the breakfast menu wasn't enough.

Never knowing if your trip was major or local by choice
Never tuned in to your personal thoughts or your roadside voice
Our time of togetherness maintained through a steady pace
Your desire to skip breakfast a saving grace.

Near the end of my trip you suddenly said goodbye
No smiles of joy or tears of relief did I cry
My vision continuously focused upon the restaurant straight ahead
As the 26 footer left the road putting our brief liaison to bed.

MY LAMP IS LOW

Trying valiantly to blow out the candles on my cake
Some gifts to open for the givers who cannot wait
Wrinkles growing on my face representing both moments of triumph and despair
Reaching to touch the top of my head where there once was hair.

Moments now etched in memory upon my soul
Mistakes I made; times when I seemed out of control
A few memories when my star shined bright
Reliving the past often kept me up at night.

Watching our youth as the heirs of the next generation
High technology coupled with protest seems to monopolize their concentration
Solutions may lie in relating to the echoes of the past
Sadly my next trip to the hospital may turn out to be my last.

THE ONLY ONE

The recipient of an emotionally charged communiqué led the innocent ones away
A threat born out of frustration showed mental health normalcy on hold today
Trapped alone inside his emotional shell as confused as he could be
She alone of all the people came to sit with me.

Management promised the recipient all the protection available, the Pentagon even too
No male on the payroll today is permitted to poison the environment belonging to you
Calling up another monarch to handle the problematic behavior that came to be
She alone of all the people came to sit with me.

A year passed by as the innocent ones attempted to regain the status quo
An environment of permanent division on unification could never embrace so
The innocent one moved with grace part of her growing legacy
Meanwhile a lonely supporter alone of all the people came to sit with me.

Now with the passage of time memories have turned to ashes and dust
A monarch shouts out his shortcomings upon the staleness of leadership crust
Walking for my friend now so difficult as the day that came to be
She alone of all the people came to sit with me.

MILESTONES

A first born expected in the new year delivered on a day of thanks
To a young East European couple added to the ranks
Facing the challenge of growth during post war normalcy
Along with every day expenses and small paying job dependency.

Disciplined from the beginning on the first day of school
Pushed hard to succeed following the concepts of the golden rule
A summer graduation the result of sacrifice and family endeavors
So proud yet so humble as a recipient of the first college degree letter.

Signing up for four years so youthful and trim
Assigned to a large sea going vessel though the young man could not swim
A war time and peace time cruise attached to his resume
Subjected to more danger through a riot than the Communists could offer in their war time play.

Handicapped on paper though able to help others lead a better life
Offered employment security along with the daily subjection to arguments and strife
Now told by many I've been here too long
Time to make preparations for a graceful exit to the sounds of a retirement song.

Many avenues available now in a twenty four hour day
Time to entice old friends to come out and play
A glance at the obituary page to see familiar names passing away
Along with the gray hair and wrinkles a nearly completed life now on display.

A PARTICIPANT IN A LONG LINE OF PATIENCE

Pushing a cart holding a few staples in the direction of the express line
In terms of minutes a quick exit hoping to find
An irate customer makes noise over a price check in front of me
The recipient of a front row seat sadly I see.

Another patron produces a credit card that won't work
Across my face sadness, laughter, and then a smirk
Perhaps instead of paying for the food I decided to steal
At least in the jail cell I'd receive a fair deal.

Waiting a length of time for a bank employee to say a friendly hello
Late arrivals hoping to move ahead of me challenging my temper to blow
Hearing a sad story about the loss of some money
For a hard working member of the middle class a temporary defeat though not very funny.

A Family Judicial Decision

Somewhat nervous being introduced to the family as her new beau
Looks of skepticism made me feel less than welcomed as the neighborhood's new show
Initial conversation centered around vocational choice and future commitment plans
Amid centers of privacy family members took turns demeaning my candidacy as their sister's
new man.

His color much too pale, his emotional fortitude completely hidden from view
On the checklist of basics certainly not the right man for you
Perhaps connecting through a hidden ploy called desperation
His background certainly worthy of a complete family investigation.

My intended caught in the middle with bombs bursting in air
On the subject of frogs and lemons falsely a recipient of more than her fair share
Holding me at a quiet moment not willing to acknowledge the voices of despair
A voice barely above a whisper; "On the offer of your committed love I'll always share"

Ode To An Old Man

Aware of your vision from your table you cast upon me
Another old man in quest of romantic sympathy
A young girl waiting on tables to earn some hard needed cash
Not held hostage to your extra tip money, or your silent verbal line trash.

Your hard life behind you certainly no fault of mine
The chosen ones who misunderstood your feeble attempts to be kind
The present state of lonliness for your information so fatal to many
The quest for intercession in my private life not worth a single shiny penny.

Your hopeless dreams died at the entrance to this trendy food eatery
The manager warned us about these rituals my first day on the payroll you see
Time to separate from each other along the lines of a permanent peaceful guarantee
Seniors to their own generation must be loyal in search of all valuable commodities.

HER CURIOSITY

Gently asking the cashier about the book in her hand
To my surprise about the author she stated she knew the talented man
Coming in for some food and then saying goodbye
His wisdom on these pages teaching me how to laugh and how to cry.

So simple and quiet a person of humble taste
Displaying constantly through his words; "A mind is a tragic thing to waste"
"Can I meet him?"; "My approach will be sound"
His reaction to me a humble smile or an unforgiving frown.

The wrinkles and hair loss symbols of knowledge gained through the ages
Mood swings amid everyday occurrences found in abundance upon his life in stages
When you meet him thoughts upon another poem he may write
Your presence with respect for him a most welcome sight.

ALL THE CREDIT BELONGS TO ME

Coming into a new office with a resume a mile long
My job qualifications to the world seem very strong
Telling everyone else their skills are limited or non existent in scope
Put me on the payroll I am your only hope.

My residency with a company always seems to last three years or so
My bosses seem to display a consistency in letting me go
Very involved in taking on the projects of others and then turning them around
On the question of failure upon my shoulders I never make a sound.

Always telling the truth whenever I'm on the phone
Outside interests can always contact me on company time from their own time zone
The best thing that ever happened to your company by far
Everybody loves me as the establishment's number one star.

TREATS FOR THE CHILDREN

Measuring carefully my receptiveness to sugar and salt
High numbers create health issues where my system will balk
My search successfully connected with snack foods known as rice cakes by name
Tasting so sweet I almost felt normal just the same.

Eager to share my discovery I connected with an admirer in the early morn
For her young ones a new taste experiment was born
Her happiness exhibited by a warm smile displayed from ear to ear
My offering was accepted in a manner so wonderfully clear.

Now another flavor for her is on the line
A sweet taste for vegetables now I must find
Presently on the plate always pushing away
Sweet flavored rice snacks on the menu always small voices seem to say.

A DOWNWARD SPIRAL TO OBLIVION

The death of a relative dropped an unexpected amount of abundance in his lap
The number in the will affected him emotionally where he sat
Off to the races was he with the people he knew before
From the low man on the roster to the CEO of his own financial store.

Constantly reminding his friends of the new position he was at
Repairing personal issues of hardship took precedent over those in need at the local laundermat
Showing off his new toys to soon to be former friends now an irritating diversion
For those on the edge of falling into poverty characterized submersion.

Before long those in his acquaintance wanted to forget about him
Instead of a green lined wallet I liked his other half identical twin
Now alone in emotional captivity with the material tools of his trade
Taking the wrong turn in a journey toward respectability telling the world he had it made.

LIKE A MOSQUITO

Circling noisily around my ear
Searching hungrily for a place upon the skin coated runway so abundantly clear
In quest of a bloated bloody feast
The little viper during the Summer an annoying beast.

Little red lumps upon my skin your calling card
Using both hands to scratch away your misery in my back yard
Quickly running to the store to purchase some protection by name
Sitting in the shade your relatives attack me just the same.

Scratching the battlefield my blood only mine to give
Your determination to connect with me a short live to live
Time after time annually year after year
Satisfying your appetite upon us available human characters without any fear.

MIGRATION

Our little ones now grown have moved away
Health costs have escalated putting additional strain upon our retirement pay
Dad looks upon Mom; Mom looks upon Dad
After many years pulling up roots is emotionally sad.

Friendly neighbors no longer visable from our backyard
Rising property taxes make the challenge of daily living very hard
Realator brokers fill our mailboxes up with silly messages every day
"Time to sell and move on when the market is favorable," They all seem to say.

We look to the South where hurricanes visit every other week
We look to the heartland where tornados are often at their peak
We look to the North with no veto power over the snow
Maybe the dry weather of Arizona holds the promise for our future aspirations to go.

Senior citizen homes may offer us comfort galore
The casinos of Las Vegas may offer us bankruptcy and little more
After thinking and thinking and thinking some more
Our present day residence may offer us our best golden years score.

MY HOME TOWN

Street cars moving slowly down the main street of the thorofare
My little hand held in Dad's who handled all family cares
Watching a steam shovel move large amounts of dirt under the construction game
Today just a large hole, in the future the Garden State Parkway by name.

A trip around the block to look at a window filled with toys
Two blocks away the bakery gave off aromas to fill the lungs of many a little boy
In the neighborhood a newspaper store offering Tasty Pies and Chocolate Egg Cream
A weekly desire so sweet and supreme.

Two movie theaters for 25 cents to occupy my Saturday afternoons.
Birthday parties during my early years offering gifts, cake, and popping balloons
The fountain with the paper cup 10 cents and two straws for a cheap date
In the future with working papers a better opportunity for the young lady I would compensate.

Sleigh riding on the hill by the hospital that is no more
Due to rising costs reluctantly soon to close its doors
Playing Walter Mitty type baseball in the driveway for the neighbors quite a show
Among the memories of my youth so may years ago.

INSTANT STATUS

A common guy lost among many faces in the crowd
Resigned to an average life style in silence, not one to make statements outloud
Then the unexpected as six lucky numbers came out on his side
Time to sound the trumpets to show off his winning pride.

Clothes, a new set of wheels, some trendy locations to visit
Now empowered to advise others "How to get with it"
Before a married to his couch stay at home type of guy
Now a constant recipient of female proposals, visual eye contact, and desperate breathtaking sighs.

Hardly able now to keep his feet on the ground
His main competition looking for handouts or mildly disturbed whenever he's around
Always happy full of confidence never displayed by our idol before
May he always be standing upon solid ground in the future never over a trap door.

Anna And The Ape: A Love Story

A phony promotion attracted her as a means to eat
Inspired by a writer aboard ship willing to accept a back row seat
An island off the map offering her pain as the ultimate sacrifice
Captivating a large gorilla prior to his final demise.

Prehistoric creatures constantly attacked her and the crew
Saved repeatedly by her new social interest prior to delivery to the Broadway Zoo
Lured into a trap not of her making
Her tears displayed the true feelings her heart toward him was taking.

In captivity upon stage the eighth wonder was focused upon by many
His anger concentrated upon a continuation of a love alliance with one for which he was ready
At the top of the tallest building a love affair played out its final moments to a tragic end
In death a permanent love bond unlike some humans the loss of a real friend.

Homeward Bound

Upon arrival at the airport my extended family joyously awaiting me
Offering forth signs, balloons, smiles amid encouraging words of sympathy
"So happy and thankful to have you home again"
"May peaceful ventures in the future become your closest friend".

Fast asleep aboard the aircraft during the long journey home
Subjected to verbal abuse and worse from peace demonstrators while wanting to be left alone
A reluctant family member accompanied me along with radio news commenting on political division
Future comments on national policy with others a constant debatable collision.

Assisted by medical personnel during my departure from the plane
Leaving an arm and a leg behind in service to my country a gesture some labeled insane
I saw the look of sadness in my girlfriend the tears in her eyes
Half a man was returning home to her a consolation prize.

The first few nights asleep again in my bed
Waking up and screaming over reoccurring thoughts of captivity inside my head
Continuing thoughts of pain and suffering in an environment never saying goodbye
Those once close to me with words unspoken shaking their heads ready to cry.

A horse drawn carriage slowly bringing my casket into view
The somber looks upon the faces of my son and daughter about a mother they hardly knew
The campaign for equality slowly pushed me in the direction of a combat zone
A roadside explosion ended my campaign enabling me to make a final journey home.

Alarm Clock Wanted

Sounds of blissful satisfaction bouncing off the ceiling so high
Not remembering to the TV last night if I said goodbye
Another day of labor on the schedule for me
Under restful constraints unable to get up in defense of family financial security.

A small band of breakfast pilgrims in a circle do meet
Their feelings about their mentor filled with criticism and deceit
As idle moments move on removed from their natural flow
Ready and willing to tell their comatose chieftain where he can go.

Once reunited the program will return to a venue of normalcy
Early morning plans will not fall victim to a ritual of duplicity
Loyal forces will once again try the early morning menu on for size
The owners will regain a measure of appreciation in their customer's eyes.

Another Blockade In The Morning

Red lights shining creating temporary boundary lines
Traffic too small in stature to create the misery that binds
A working tourist on a temporary visit from another state
Drove his tractor trailer under a low overpass another act of fate.

Perhaps he was tired; perhaps he could not read his map
Maybe being late for his destination in his haste trying to close the gap
In need of assistance awaiting the arrival of a pickup truck from Ford
After 75,000 layoff notices perhaps a late entry not ready to get on board.

Working as a team into reverse the rig is bound to move
The roof somewhat damaged; the driver now trying to regain his groove
Local law officials filling out paperwork; a cup of coffee for today's new hero
The level of inconvenience for late arrivals as the mayor likes it at the number zero.

Nobody Really Knew Who Had Died

A band of brothers bonding together for a political ride
In search of votes not compromising the truths they held inside
Cold War Ideology mixed with social upheaval to create a lasting storm
Out of the continuing confrontation a policy for peace was born.

Accepting the voices of protest to break up big city machines
The policy of guns and butter hindered the growth of unification dreams
Women pushed forward as the vanguard of disfranchised players
New widows created daily as war time statistics came out in layers.

A final motorcade found justice in the presence of a grassy knoll
A labor issue served as a pretext for complete equality now out of control
Moving through a hotel pantry riding the success of acceptance on victory night
Suddenly the painful acceptance of finality a cold damp remorseful sight.

In mourning our losses the nation reluctantly said goodbye
At the pinnacle of development their loyal chieftains could only remember and cry
The foundation of the disconnected temporarily alive now again under wraps
No direction to follow with the final playing of taps.

Conversations: Cut & Dried
/ Compromise Not Included

Attempting to respond to the phrase; "We don't talk anymore"
Sitting together in a peaceful setting behind closed doors
Statements offered forth on the early days of my life
Opportunities passed over the basis for present day strife.

The other side repeating the formative years a time for study
A time to avoid classmates and their behavior so nutty
My rebuttal; relationships through experience take time to develop and grow
Not the result of an on/off button as the admission ticket to the big show.

A response comes forth "I raised you the wrong way"
"In my latter years how much emotional guilt do you want me to pay?"
Slowly I attempt to explain the ongoing element of change
Flexability affords social apostles the benefits of a much wider range.

Told repeatedly to venture forth and try
Not all of the available females will offer you a final goodbye
Selectivity by both sides keeps potential soul mates apart
Never to see the light of happiness always moving hopelessly in the dark.

50 Years Of Lifetime Experiences

As a young one hearing stories from your parents about a far off land
An opportunity for growth and fulfillment at your command
Situated in a neighborhood among people much like your very own
Actively seeking the benefits of life under freedom's enduring song.

Thoughts of the future when falling in love
Emotions and feelings soaring on the wings of a white dove
After a period of time fulfillment was a dream not to be
The pain of separation softened by the support of friends in sympathy.

A lifetime vocation afforded a second opportunity for one always looking so young
The bells of happiness in your honor again ready to be rung
Now solidarity is part of the program at the mid century of your life
With the anticipation of continued years of laughter and sadness, serenity and strife.

The Reciprocator

Offering a smile along with a friendly hello
Sending forth a message of acceptance; part of the humanity show
Through the highway of your heart promoting understanding and joy
Not taking part in the games of bigotry and hate and other unproductive emotional toys.

Bringing forth gifts of sweetness along with the gentleness of your soul
Allowing the world to notice the values of acceptance under your control
Not interested in the tokens of materialism from the world on the outside
Happy to share internal feelings as an example of personal pride.

Promoting selectivity as a commandment of your secret social order
Holding yourself higher on the scale of supremacy along your social border
Offering pain and hostility to those you see beneath you on a larger degree
Your personal crusade for happiness and fulfillment to the majority an ongoing mystery.

Heartache On A Small Scale

Just twelve short days after saying your final goodbyes
You initiated contact once again without using a secret disguise
Lamenting lightly about my absence at your final affair
A little late in my book for you to say you really care.

Pain once delivered sometimes never fades completely away
Hidden deep inside a psyche deposit box always to stay
My devotion always offered forth never acknowledged by you
Till the end in honor of the rules of favoritism you remained always true.

Now we travel separately along the paths chosen by us years before
After nearly seven years of unfulfilled endings we both know the score
No matter in the future how many more mountains we shall climb
Our names mentioned in passing conversation beginning with "Once upon a time"

March Madness: A Prelude To Financial Sadness

A new owner of grid sheets safely nestled in my hands
Under the spell of cheerleaders and colorful indoor bands
Asked to pick some winners in the many games they play
Not an expert by any means just earning the right to have my say.

Going along with the crowd; "Will the luck of the Irish come my way?"
Back home afraid to face the bill collectors when they want their pay
Lottery tickets mixed in with scratch offs now this madness thing comes along
Later on will I be singing an Irish victory march or the sad notes of a bankruptcy song?

Everyone lines up when I receive my check on payment day
Functioning actively with pieces of plastic I create additional delay
Afraid to admit I see no solution to this creative mess
Hooked on easy money opportunities for the rest of my life I guess.

My Medication: Out Of Sinc

A recipient of health care as a result of service to our great nation
A victim of confusion not of my creation
In need of medication to pursue the century mark
The bureaucracy meanwhile offers forth excuses looking for a place to park.

My pills sometimes too many sometimes too few
Please call this number the only thing to do
Bring an empty bottle in for a few extras lying around
No comments about your treatment always safe always sound.

Try making an appointment whenever we can fit you in
Not eligible for some medication perhaps you have a twin
If your level of dissatisfaction ever reaches a new personal high
Sign up with a new country then we can say goodbye.

Got A Light

My system signals additional cravings for nicotine
Strangers represent opportunities to fulfill my latest comfort dream
Waving a greenback in pursuit of a few puffs
My lungs will let me know somehow when I've had enough.

Someone discussing her addictive history with a friend
Regular brands, filtertip, and menthol flavored for her a real Godsend
Every morning in the course of conversation blowing off smoke
Leaving her trademark on the ground too timid to break the yoke.

Higher taxes continuously levied on this habit so bad
The pain of withdrawal for stressful people always so sad
Carry some matches or a lighter in your pocket
Your reputation as a provider will take off like a rocket.

Help Wanted

By the dawns early light expected to be here
So many small tasks to do so emphatically clear
Menus along with prices to learn; the habits of customers too
For the old men at the counter knowing exactly what to do.

Tables and countertops along with making the cash register ring
In good times during the trip to the bank the owners will sing
Washing some dishes may ruin your hands
Soiled by representatives from many foreign lands.

Hours so early the compensation really not so great
The warmth of your smile will determine your economic fate
Knowledge is power with many numbers inside your head
If your spirit isn't willing we'll quietly put your application to bed.

T. G. I. M.

Late in the afternoon with resignation present in your eyes
Exchanging pleasantries with your co-workers a 48 hour goodbye
You hear their conversations so many exciting things to do
With nothing on your personal agenda the next two days seem relatively blue.

In the evening with the TV blasting you fall asleep in your easy chair
The last thing you remember a little green reptile talking about insurance rates so unfair
In the morning when you wake up you're going for a walk
Maybe running into the mailman with whom you'll have a talk.

Coming home you read the paper, take the trash out too
The TV schedule looks empty; bouncing a ping pong ball off the wall will have to do
In the afternoon calling up a friend a memory remembered fondly with pride
A ritual repeated every Saturday during the four years since she died.

During the evening hours your thoughts wander to good music and dance
Your rejection level so heavy not willing to take another chance
In the morning you travel to your place of worship to meditate and pray
Safely carried through another weekend period referred to as Saturday.

In the late afternoon you focus on your wardrobe; the items in your briefcase too
For your boss in loyalty the proper thing to do
With the setting of the sun another 48 hours has come and gone
Feeling the emotions of joyful anticipation with your co-workers ready again to bond.

T. G. I. F.

Monday morning a time to rejuvenate the spirit and the soul
A time for planning a time to gain control
A smile of reflection on the activities of the weekend past
The moments when you let your hair down you really had a blast.

Tuesday comes upon you to cover for the mistakes of yesterday
The week has just really started already there are bills to pay
A trip to the dentist a canal other than Panama the tooth doctor plans for you
Besides your mouth your wallet will sadly suffer too.

Wednesday brings you to the middle in pain ready to stay at home
A loyal dedicated professional not willing to leave a friend alone
Upon reception of your medication you tend to float through the day
The tooth fairy will not reimburse you; it doesn't work that way.

On Thursday you call yourself a survivor as you already know
One of many rejected applicants who wanted to be on the TV show
A pain in the foot tells you your feet are firmly anchored to the ground
No longer hooked on medication no more magic available around.

On Friday though stuck in traffic it's a very happy sound
Five additional days of commitment now you're homeward bound
Through daily trial and tribulation you passed another test
A soccor mom with laundry to do and then perhaps a little rest.

MEMORIES ABOUT MY TOES

Like most newborn infants I started out with ten
Introduced to my big toe I counted him as my first true friend
In the years that followed tight shoes took its toll
Ten was reduced to nine because of my abusive soul.

My toes to my date not a problem causing sorrow
"Together we'll get up and look for the other one tomorrow"
Nails began to crack growing inward day by day
Later on with an open shoe my neck would have to pay.

Now my toes like wild birds so curved and living off the ground
My sissors do the cutting for me a healthy sound
Through foot powder and hot water I finally find relief
On the remaining nine counting the ones I want to keep.

ONE TRACK MIND

His words like particles of sugar on a waffle I claim as mine
His location at the local library on any given day by design
Readings on literature along with new words pleasant to my ear
Holding conversations on many subjects to our collective hearts so dear.

Words exchanged as foreplay for our future expectations later in the night
The presence of exposure causing the seeds of desire to bloom so very bright
Hotel bed, car seat, or bath tub strange as it may seem
A satisfactory environment to culminate all of our erotic dreams.

A heavy presence of sweat encountered at the local gym
Without any clue to his identity I always called my new heart throb "Him"
Physical fitness was a passion I wanted to be part of
Exercising all my mental options in pursuit of one called love.

Funny lines or repeated jokes the origin of my smile
In a world often filled with cruelty for me the extra mile
Thoughts about his past I kept hidden deep inside
The search for lighter moments much easier with him as my guide.

LOST AND FOUND

Her only desire to light up and flick ashes upon the ground
A review of the weather followed with few people around
Saying goodbye to her cigarette to her work station she moved on
At the same time her memory was playing a forgetful song.

A maintenance man witnessed the shining metal upon the stoop
Expecting her to come down quickly to rediscover and regroup
In her absence a special trip for me to make
A hero's reputation was there for me to take.

In her work area the usual reason for me was not in vogue
In truth I've paid a few citations it may be told
Waving the object of my visitation her eyes slowly came to realize
In the spirit of honesty her possessions were a major prize.

Inferiority Complex

Looked down upon as a female member of a minority race
Forced to develop personal skills to create her own power base
Relying upon others to get her work done
A high title after many years her triumph over adversity painfully won.

Arriving from a country where intimidation is king
Appointing himself as a know it all on most everything
Short in stature always moving from side to side
Abusing all in his vision involuntarily along for the ride.

Paternal love resulting in bruises with the promise of more
Not always welcomed when entering through the front door
Standing on a soap box to share personal memories of long time abuse
Anxiety gains control when unpleasant thoughts are again on the loose.

His claim to a title made him travel in our direction
In terms of leadership not really worthy of our affection
Conversing with young women to chase away his separation blues
Relying upon a powerful adversary in search of survival clues.

Always a loner with no words of praise rushing to his side
Not able to converse on an elementary level concerning a proper social guide
Emotionally destroyed in an encounter with a woman once upon a time
Operating silently in the shadows of life unable ever to shine.

Major Ills Of Society

Studying the menu at the mature age of thirty five
For others the words leap out at them and come alive
Passing a library a building forever off limits to me
Just guessing at the words on the page in their total simplicity.

A young couple briefly connecting when future expectations were running high
Separating soon after; the emotional fallout matched giant hailstones falling out of the sky
Coming into the world with no father to call my very own
For me a permanent position on the suspicious highway of life in the non trusting zone.

Unwilling to fill out forms the young clerk passed out to me
Raising the bar on my side regarding personal dignity
On the time period in question with little patience ready to run
A difficult journey in quest of freedom under the unforgiving desert sun.

If Only Our Paths Had Never Crossed

If only introductions to the new arrivals were reduced by one
My sad lamenting song of regret today would never be sung
My attendance record would continue according to plan
The resulting work overload would never put my manager in a jam.

Whispering partners would never exchange words about the problem over there
My social life in the minds of others not even a single care
Like a mechanical robot focused upon a beginning then a trip to go home
Always in control of my behavior patterns when left alone.

Some of the active players have since departed the scene
Eager to follow the paths of their own personal dreams
Long ago I made up my mind to stand tall and fight
Every day in defense of my reputation I pick up a pen and I write.

The Food Emporium

Words of inspiration floating out across the room
Hunger pains of desperation bringing forth thoughts of resignation and impending gloom
The call goes out to a major eatery located in the center of town
Send forth a delivery of major league caliber where hungry appetites abound.

The major flow of knowledge never reaches the inner circle of competing minds
A parent child membership in many households never one that really binds
An academic challenge often pushed over to the side
The fast food empire of the local business merchants the only one that guides.

Graduation Day arrives with the wearing of cap and gown
Four sizes larger now since your physique goes round and round
Never a college campus are you able to explore
A look of anticipation at the help wanted sign upon the local fast food restaurant's door.

LATE NIGHT ARRIVAL

The sentinel at the front door peered out into the night
A weary traveler was home again a most welcome sight
Unloading food, a few yawns, plus a sleeping bag too
Inquiring about her favorite TV show out of the blue.

Keeping an eye on the family in various locations a responsibility with little fun
The job a lifetime occupation always active never completely done
Words of endearment offered to turn a lifestyle upside down
Sparks always begin flying when more than one generation seeks common ground.

As the one in the middle always willing to say good night
A few rounds of verbal skirmishing another non-communicating fight
An early departure planned in the morning as one has to let go
With no agreement on the horizon the combatants always determined to remain foes.

GASSED OUT BY GASOLINE

Numbers at the pump rising so high
No stopping point in sight as they touch the sky
Vacation plans for this year interrupted once again
Local activities on the agenda program like a long lost friend.

Middle East connections very busy counting their profits during the Summer Season
Chief Magistrates in Washington with a wink think there must be a reason
Price gauging and long lines are with us to stay
Changes in conservation plans are necessary without delay.

Alternative fuel ideas still bottled up too controversial to be let loose
Big Oil through their legal eagles wants to postpone this profit abuse
Highway passage for cars the usual way to travel
Everyone turns to bicycles as their recreational pursuits begin to fade and unravel.

Preparations For A Departure

The office hierarchy came together in the spirit of celebration
Throwing verbal hand grenades against each other they fashioned a new social creation
Soliciting food donations, money, and signatures upon a card
Trying with great determination inside four walls to duplicate the local back yard.

Among the missing notables a few had other things to do
During the passing reign they labored with professional dedication always so true
Local ladies banged their heads, ran around, and somehow got things right
For the privilege of telling next of kin about their lousy day later on that night.

The departing leader graciously gave out words of joy along with hugs for all
Taking mental notes on the absentees their promotions in the future to forestall
With a final look around moving down the ramp toward the exit for the final time
Tears of joy mixed with tears of sadness she now can claim them all as mine.

Speculation

A relic of an enterprise located upon a mainstream corner of hope
A money making venture for the average consumer larger in scope
Hoping for the removal of a wasteful interior; a visual remorseful decay
Thousands more labor hours required before the arrival of appetites ready to play.

Food is the fuel with added sweetness for the soul
Not handled properly by an obese populace sometimes raging out of control
Pulling their wrinkled dollars out of their extra large faded jeans
Displaying a round the clock constant hunger ready to burst out at the seams.

Verbal thoughts on the future offered forth by the mainstays on the block
Ready to gather at a new watering hole to show their brethren what they've got
Asking questions on the issue making the doorman part of the puzzle too
A white bag carrying flotilla the advance guard of the future consumption crew.

Addiction

Too many compliments about my new physique ringing in my ears
Not ready for the attention; not ready for the cheers
Held hostage by the baked goods section of a local neighborhood food store
After one sample of calorie filled pastry I was ready for more.

The weather was too cold for exercise to grab hold of me
Rice cakes joined the daily menu becoming part of my diet filled fantasy
A tire I once said goodbye to regained a foothold of my soul
Calories like snowflakes descended upon me as I struggled for control.

The food groups pyramid from the local medical center buried forever in my room
Additional pounds of heaviness created a resignation like gloom
In front of a mirror somehow gaining strength to observe my foe
"In which direction in the near future will my attitude go?"

Too Old To Make A Difference

Reluctant eyes cast upon my head where vibrant hair once used to grow
Heavy breathing offered forth by one with wild oats still to sow
Her friends commenting with mock surprise that her grandfather had come to town
A major find in Archeology; not one for the youthful crowd to have around.

My virtues once explained did little to clear the air
Comments about her old boyfriends came forth with whom to compare
After a few hours my yawning covers the memories I carry alone inside
Memories became my anchor as any thoughts for acceptance long ago had died.

Alone in the early hours of a new day our mutual thoughts sense the end has come
Feeble attempts for continuity admit our future is empty without mutual feelings of fun
Lines and creases have created pieces where once solidarity reigned supreme
Better to go our separate ways rather than living out the expectations of an empty dream.

Requiem For A Parking Lot

Parking my vehicle safely between the lines
Successfully avoiding "No Parking" zones as well as numerous traffic fines
Pushing myself with energy toward the center of town
Several errands to be run; legs please don't let me down.

Stopping inside the grocery store now and then
High prices soon made me invisible the usual economic trend
Thinking on my own the store would soon have to go
Instead the corporate structure decided to promote a much bigger show.

Now my safe concrete haven is no more
Searching desperately for parking my anger growing at the core
Never planning to visit again the store now part of history
Cruising along the streets in search of space now a continuing misery.

The Few/ The Proud/ The Unhappy

Visual interpretation of empty chairs decorating an empty room
Applicants in quest of services their expectations not quite ready to swoon
Few defenders of the present day oratory ready to assist
Too many holes in the total package; something's gone amiss.

Some searching elsewhere ready to leave town
Some hindered by financial restraints; for the rest of their lifetimes still locally bound
Cuts in services again coming down the pike
Relief in the form of new faces and new leadership nowhere in sight.

People accepting the idea of a day off every two weeks
Ready to make a difference seated at home in their favorite TV seat
Early risers continue their effort based upon the character of their mind
Their strong sense of devotion like a magical capsule so difficult to find.

Old time fossils trying to relate to the new kids on the block
New age technology going head to head with the ghosts of Woodstock
"Will the noise of despair ever reach an agreeable end?"
"Or will the silence of understanding cover the rebellious pilgrims once again my friend?"

TRIFECTA 1934

Outlaws were once known as heroes across an economically ravaged land
Robbing banks while shooting those offering law and order a helping hand
Out of Washington came the order to track the desperadoes down
No bank throughout the country was safe as long as they were around.

A lady in red helped bring a famous lawbreaker down
A tip to the authorities acknowledged he was in town
After the movie it was too late to run
Collective firepower ended Public Enemy Number One's criminal fun.

Another legend was located in the corn attempting to get away
Three bullets found the mark another golden day
The press created a hero out of the void where there once was none
Reluctantly pushed into the spotlight the public now had one.

Again around Thanksgiving the agent reached his peak
Another gang member absorbed some lead and took a final seat
The bureau office in Washington would not completely accept the work in review
The emerging hostility in years to come for the lonely hero never ever having a clue.

LIMITATIONS

No sports star on the playing field destined to be
The family's ongoing disappointment manufactured in their continuing hostility
My grade point average too low with little attention paid to books
The mirror on the wall communicates back to me my less than average looks.

No field trips on the horizon planning to take
Fire damage so comprehensive on my last endeavor toward baking a cake
The body shop is trying to repair the family car
After dad handed over the keys to the family's number one star.

Trapped inside an elevator the fire department received a call
The family together in unison asked why they bothered at all
Caught up in the hobby of shoplifting I failed to make bail
Two months have passed by with no guests visiting me here at the jail.

69

Versailles 1919

Too many casualties for a nation to beare
The issue of compensation became a major affair
National self preservation would readjust the boundaries under claim
Another nation regarding the origin several years before would accept all the blame.

The balance of power on the continent pushed forward amid a flu epidemic type disease
An island nation determined to maintain freedom of the seas
Air raids along with rationing for the local populace created a somber tone
Peacetime economics on the basis of new technology upon old traditions found a new home.

An economic power found the sentiments for isolation very strong
Reconstructing the peace for Congress and the President both sides always somewhat wrong
Progressive ideas for the future facing a reactionary pattern of thought
Idealism would never carry the day for the spoils the victors sought.

The class struggle would replace the old system based upon privilege and material gain
Nobles along with peasants, workers, and intelligentsia would all share the pain
Guerrilla warfare would advance the idea of a totalitarian state
Upon the ashes of a conflict just ended a new dictatorship would cast its fate.

Over Before It Began

Eager to share with you my episodes of everyday painful living
At home and in the workplace the people always so unforgiving
Your receptive ear always giving me courteous common sense advice
Grateful to share early morning encounters with someone so very nice.

Two years of bonding between us has reached a plateau of no return
Separation between us is necessary as you shall shortly learn
Crossing a boundary line caused a red flag to appear in front of my face
Time to bring this affair to a meaningful conclusion without a trace.

Past encounters inside my psyche have left a residue of pain
A man of good intentions like yourself is not to blame
Allow me to continue my journey through the wilderness of lonesome town
Where women hurting individuals armed with destructive thoughts are never found.

SNIPER ATTACK

My work assignments placed in a cabinet location by design
Easy access for reference needs in the future hoping to find
Suddenly a personal phone call I must be willing to take
Through the crosshairs of his rifle the assassin played for high stakes.

Without uttering a word my administrative work was ripped up and destroyed
He with great political clout taking advantage of a little boy
I protested in a loud voice to the powers that be
My assailant pointed to his chin, laughing while continuing to make fun over me.

My positive feelings for the office from that point were never more
Political liaisons held the upper hand while I held the lower score
Since that time to insults developing a heavy armor of skin
Subjected to continuing political abuse in a high stakes game never hoping to win.

AN OFFICE OF ONE

Open solicitation of the hierarchy for the project at hand
Offering dedication in pursuit of success for the higher command
After visitation information brought back for all to share
A rebel in hiding brought forth more pressure than I could possibly beare.

Lining up support a product of her evil mind
Her state of unhappiness to most others labeled her the hurting kind
False accuisations pushed forth against me causing negative duress
A hoped for successful project reduced now to a big mess.

Later on in privacy confessing all I knew
The matriarch of the family once again in the dark without a clue
These moments registered in my memory bank come the holiday season
An empty chair present among the celebrants for a very special reason.

POCKETS

Traveling along an academic journey to a Southern border state
In quest of vocational proficiency my dreams could not wait
As the oldest my graduation fulfilled my family destiny
Fill another pocket for me.

Signing up for a tour of duty along the way
Like my father I thought our way of life was democratically OK
As the oldest my military service stood out on the family tree
Fill another pocket for me.

A new government program out of Washington came into my view
Born out of hypocricy so noble and true
Six months later separated from your duties with little fanfare and free
Twenty eight years after your erroneous prediction fill another pocket for me.

I NEED YOUR HELP I THINK

Running into me in the early morn to you quite a shock
Upon hearing my boring words of conversation you wished you owned a rock
Suddenly in my direction a favor you did ask
Happening to me many times over the years quite a simple task.

I mentioned words like resume and an application for you to fill
You wanted no part of this assignment for me a bitter pill
You told me you were tired success would take some time
Another act of gamesmanship the aggrevation would be all mine.

If you are sincere responsibility from you is also due
If you are playing, a mutual gift of permanent separation is also true
Stop trying to read between the lines on issues of mine you do not know
A solution to your problem only possible with mutual cooperation making it so.

The Pyramid Of Attachment

The joy of connection a common campus sight
A mutual feeling of trust and cooperation the way to get things right
Spending time in person along with hours of exchanging pleasantries through the phone
On thoughts of separation not willing to leave the other party alone.

Some weekends we spend together as unity becomes the key
Enduring moments of comic silliness along with heavy discussions on philosophy
Drawing closer together mixing moments of sadness with larger periods of fun
Drawing a mutual conclusion for each other; this person may be the one.

On one knee I made a proposal offering forth a small box containing a token of permanent
glitter inside
Tears of acceptance in your eyes forming a common union built upon devotion and pride
Months of preparation lie ahead in creating a special day filled with joy
Always dreaming of this time when I was a little boy.

In our state of matrimonial bliss our family expanded by a few
We spent years developing understanding on issues we hardly knew
Changing jobs and buying houses our feet constantly on the move
In the spirit of solidarity trying to find and maintain our groove.

Disunity affected our garden of love as money got in the way
In-laws from opposing sides made their presence known determined to have their say
A trial separation made freedom a gift for our mutual souls
Saying goodbye to one another with dignity; trying to maintain control.

Upon hearing of my passing, "Did you take time out to reflect and to cry?"
Tears of sadness upon the issues together we could not decide
Trying hard to measure up as a husband, a father, and a man
A ray of bright light amid the turmoil still trying to understand.

LOVE: PIECES OF THE PUZZLE

Seeing you for the first time a moment of magic
If you are not available a temporary loss really not tragic
Along with your height and your smile the tools certainly are all there
With no other woman on earth would I willingly share.

Introducing myself after seeing you from a distance a few times
My words covered my nervousness fueled by the sounding of chimes
Telling others about words of affection wisdom certainly making my day
Secretly hoping on future summer evenings you and I would have opportunities to play.

Thoughts on you cover the waking hours of my morning normal load
Deciding to make a move for the chance of striking gold
Believing in myself a vision of victory within my sight
Though the ride may have its ups and downs I have to hold on tight.

Sitting together at a table we discover some common things to do
Allowing each other breathing space while believing in our common union now so true
Holding hands walking down the street a look of ecstasy upon our faces
The warmth of our togetherness even non visionary loners can see the traces.

In a common private setting feelings locked up are now coming into view
My comfort zone is very high as long as I'm with you
Believing through this ritual I've finally made the grade
In my past I've had my moments; my dues have all been paid.

GOING IN CIRCLES

Stating your timetable out loud for the weekend at hand
Another action packed situation relating to the playoff dominating sports' plan
Out of the blue a verbal hint for a change
A little difficult at the last possible minute to rearrange.

Words of regret and wisdom thrown out to the other side
Not ready to admit guilt with the tools of communication as a guide
Amid raising voices both parties ready to admit personal despair
Unable to agree on a compromise though ready to promote hostility plus a threatening glare.

Every time possible the voices of silence close the lines of understanding down
"My way is the only way"; the dominant theme in town
Aside from the competitors one wonders if an impartial arbitrator can be found
To properly balance the scales of justice when situations of this type come around.

THE SAME OLD SONG

Reluctantly boarding a train for a familiar trip again
Punished continuously for a sincere attempt to acquire another friend
Marching slowly along the road to a well remembered destination
Another academic entity a product of their non favorites penalizing creation.

Ready to listen to the sounds of the old familiar tune
A just dessert for weak personalities unable to make available women swoon
Reading printed words upon paper plus a knowledgeable video too
In the future avoiding women at all costs the proper thing to do.

Never again will their verbal lies afford them power to humiliate me
A spineless victim of their secretly creative fatal gossip manufacturing dynasty
Now the hierarchy rests upon the waves of anticipation for another wrong move
Too sophisticated in my isolation to ever attempt another connection so crude.

MY ORDEAL

A combination of cheesecake and tuna fish attacked my system one day
Heavy sweating coupled with stomach upheaval took control as onlookers began to pray
An EMT Squad arrived as agony increased the score
Soon I was headed toward an ambulance parked outside my front door.

"Where are we going?" as IV's attached themselves to my veins
Hopefully to a quiet location of medicinal magic removed from the local cars, buses, and trains
For six hours upon my stretcher only pain and dryness accompanied me
With no nurses around a sympathetic doctor assisted me in a journey to the local lavatory.

After an ultrasound the medical personnel figured out what was wrong
A local doctor advised toothpaste to improve my stale breath like song
A procedure removed a stone as sleeping for me never permitted a wink
After a few more days ready for the morgue though my chart said I was in the pink.

Soon my gall bladder and me had a permanent parting of the ways
Losing pounds with hospital food leading me through the maze
Walking through the halls an exercise to help the passing of time
Awakened at all hours by the blood brigade their thoughts on me so divine.

With a high temperature my departure was delayed day by day
I threatened to remain through the holidays so everyone would have to pay
The doctor saw the futility so graciously he gave up the fight
Allowing my departure a much thinner version of my usual healthy sight.

SEE YOU AT SEVEN

Thoughts of contentment wrapped up in my boyfriend's arms
Casting a weary eye on the clock, held hostage by his numerous charms
Not trying to act silly rather as one of the wise
Time to part company tomorrow early to rise.

Dropped off by a family member I made it on time
Showing up late would reduce my reputation to just a solitary little dime
My boss expected four ladies but had to settle for me
Inside his anger was boiling over the absence of the missing three.

Moving swiftly between tables I put on a professional company smile
One I practiced in front of a mirror for quite a long while
Offering forth menus for all our patrons to see
My mentor meanwhile was busy offering forth apologies to everyone in the galaxy.

Loyalty is part of the creed in the corporation zone
Acts of indifference reduce the ability of our profit making tone
Always there for the top brass to witness my arrival in their line of vision
Unlike the others there trying extra hard to make a smooth like transition.

DEADLY MISCHIEF

A little boy and girl walking along the street a future date with destiny
Dressed up in their usual school apparel finery
Perhaps thinking about the long weekend soon to be
Relating to other family members in many forms of spontaneous gaiety.

Another little boy for the long weekend not really planning that far
An act of negativity today would make him a star
Gaining unlawful access he set the wheels of death in motion
Unaware of the consequences perhaps causing a front page commotion.

In a matter of seconds the little girl was no more
Trapped by the weight of the mechanized beast amid the tragedy it bore
A few days before in the principal's office a declaration of punishment was forsaken
As a result of this omission sadly an innocent life was taken.

The Smallest Seed In The Lettuce Patch

Humble and silent inside the envelope purchased at the farmer's store
The odds against reaching maturation discussed behind a closed door
United with the soil during the windy days of Spring
Pushing a successful crop towards the heavens for the psyche the best of everything.

Nursed along in the spirit of confidence by a soil maiden avoiding stress
In the morning greeting violators in a legal atmosphere under great duress
Back at home soil, air, water, and sun had their way
As the non green thumb segment of the populace at the store had more to pay.

With the passing of time a successful crop earned the reply; "I told you so"
Photos and smiles accompanied the soil monarch unwilling to let go
Hoping for a future where a large cash crop would make gardening labors fun
Remembering that the fanfare began long ago through the choice of the smallest one.

Golden Classic

The wide body was busy composing itself in front of my place
The women inside busy going through papers as a measure of saving grace
Handcuffs attached to their belt as a means of controlling the captive genie
Working well on all captives except for a rebel named Houdini

The fortress on wheels ready to give unlucky youth a final ride down the street
Inside a cell the passage of time gives way to thoughts so strong yet so weak
Law and order a mixed group today as every one wears pants
Opening doors near the classic provide a forum for self expression or a stone like trance.

The spaciousness of the interior never intended for use as a joy ride
A final glimpse of freedom for its occupants continuously removed along with their pride
Through its darkened windows another day begins
Women again going through papers neither identical or fraternal in the form of twins.

The Pillager

Presenting oneself as a new literary sensation with style
After signing a contract ready to travel the extra mile
Putting down words on paper about a theme utilized before
After a few weeks of investigation emerging forth was the true score.

The support group once united as a sign of jubilation
Quickly disbanded upon discovering the first sign of your procrastination
Out of the spotlight your future no longer a triumphant journey for success
Into the arms of deception and intrigue seeking a welcome caress.

Future writers would have to examine the inner feelings of their soul
Enlightened words on paper a claim to ownership their's to control
A receptive public skeptical at times about the sincereity of a publication
Wondering about the emergence of a new talent through their collective fascination.

A Romantic Affair With A Pepsi Machine

A dry mouth giving off a thirst in quest of relief
Money for my salvation in my pocket do I keep
Approaching my hero I look for the slot
Then I initiate the selection process to see what he's got.

Maybe a cola or maybe just playing a hunch
Something extra sweet like Hawaiian Punch
Not really satisified by Ginger Ale or Mountain Dew
Going over all the buttons a second time before I am through.

Waiting patiently after my decision to claim my chosen prize
Passersby eye me suspiciously through innocent eyes
Turning the cap slowly I raise my bottle high
Moisture molecules slowly descend into my reservoir my silent satisfaction cry.

EVERYBODY GETS THEIR KICKS

Every four years the world stops to follow the path of a round ball
A universal game for the rich and the poor; the big and the small
Stadiums are filled with smiling faces and national colors galore
Some teams falling quickly while others have their fans cheering for more.

Work takes a holiday as the locals cheer on their heroes
Hoping after 90 minutes for at least one score leaving the opposition with nothing but zeros
Coaches are fired then rehired after a short delay
Yellow cards and red cards after penalties make aggressive teams pay.

After a month of continuous action two teams compete for the cup
Hoping that after all the pain and sacrifice their squad has enough
In the beginning the nature of the game made the world stop
After everything is said and done only ONE TEAM finished up on top.

SHARING MY MESSAGE WITH THE WORLD

Since I have an issue with people I desire an island of my own
A place of peace and reflection often called a quiet zone
Don't remind me about young men the way things used to be
Thoughts about my experiences now just a painful memory.

Proudly wearing my message on my shirt transmitting my views to the deaf and dumb
No need to listen to their cries of denial like where do they come from
Independently I chart my course the captain of my ship
Not willing to accept con artists as companions on my trip.

Many sacrifices I have made many emotions I have shone
Forcing my acceptance on the "In Crowd" much better off alone
Never forced to pay extra postage to have my message read
Reading my thoughts between the lines at this time better off unsaid.

Looking For Work To Cure My Recreational Blues

Offering myself a guilt trip I rest my weary head
Thinking outloud about the chores to do I cannot remain in bed
Starting off with house cleaning I travel next to the laundry room
Once the on switch is pushed I say goodbye to the late night evening moon.

I spend some time on breakfast a cup of coffee just a tease
To soften up my guilt trip to put my life at ease
Soon I move outside to cut my field of grass
A young slugger's latest achievement leaves me with some broken glass.

In the afternoon turning on the TV I listen to the local news
Additional horror stories have me wishing I was on a cruise
During the evening hours I have some bills to pay
Returning soon for some rest to prepare myself for another work filled day.

Reserved Parking

Empty spaces close to the store decorated in blue
Saving me steps; reserved for people like me as well as those like you
My arms filled with bundles a slip of paper awaits me on my return
Receiving a citation because of my indifference; "When will I ever learn?"

These spaces reserved for the heroes who used to be
Who defended our freedom in its hour of maximum danger now just a double amputee
The defender of the field at Bunker Hill; a survivor at Valley Forge
Who followed the leadership of a general at that time named George.

Two hundred thirty years of freedom paid for with American dead
Remembered today only on holidays so the local paper said
The time has come for me to leave the field to you
To acknowledge with gratitude your earned right to park upon the field of blue.

Requiem For A Doorknob

Human hands applying daily pressure to make an obstacle give way
Fear of possible detainment in another medium made anxious breadwinners act like this every day
Someone paid a visit in the middle of the night
Separating the instrument of mental satisfaction from the multitudes before the early light.

Morning pilgrims found bewilderment when their journey came to a sudden end
Warm thoughts of appreciation toward the doorman replaced by suspicious ones toward their
former friend
A trip inside the elevator as a silent prayer passes through their lips
Inhaling additional medication along with water providing extra sips.

The owner found a locksmith and gave him an open hand
Replace the object of all our desires to lessen the pain of my rebellious band
A look of selectivity is found in the morning look of many eyes
Fearing always the thought of possible confinement where no hears their painful cries.

Owner Of The Key

Moving slowly worn out by the burdens entrusted to her care
Producing an instrument to unlock a passageway proving she was there
The stairs a small opportunity to develop some muscle tone
Avoiding the unreliable elevator located in the danger zone.

If the passageway was locked the unreliable alternative became the plan for the day
If the passageway was open so much easier for removal of the mental impediment this way
In confidence one asked if the passageway was her only claim to fame
In reply one of several duties for a master of the game.

In my pocket several keys lay waiting ready for a momentary need
Never part of my assignment to rescue a passageway seeker with all deliberate speed
Taking care of my own business with all attention to detail
Waiting patiently for the lady of the morning with her weapon ready to sail.

BOARDWALK PLAYGROUND POWER

The longest walking track made out of wood I have ever seen
Lined up with merchants selling everything from pizza to coffee with cream
Cyclists navigating a personal path from left to right
Everywhere I look seagulls within my viewing eyesight.

Amusement rides out on the water waiting for patrons to fill
Looking for a special eatery since I have time on my hands to kill
Couples and singles move briskly in the sunlight out for a morning stroll
A few of the unfortunate holding plastic cups their future trying to control.

Souvenir stands advise the tourists in the crowd to take something home
Large neon signs push the odds of lady luck leaving poverty all alone
Tractors crossing through humanity where traffic lights are never destined to be
Adding another element of intrigue to the early morning scenery.

Construction offers confusion where a shopping mall used to be
Just like an annual beauty pageant now just a piece of history
Additional boardwalk playgrounds are available to a Summer fast lane addict like you
Travel north or south on the local highway to find your recreational clue.

SEDUCED BY THE SLOTS

Hearing about the success stories of others over a plate of breakfast cousine
Long overdue to step into the winner's circle to claim my American Dream
An early rising again with false hopes on my side
Still not willing to accept the fact these hopes long ago have died.

Long before dawn's early light my wheels are moving along the victory road
This time things will be different the bill of goods my psyche has been sold
Saying goodbye to President Jackson I again enter a familiar domain
Ten minutes later as the latest victim of poverty ready to complain.

The ritual of futility repeats itself at several machines
A hidden scream of anguish ready to burst out at the seams
Adding up the negativeity over many years when everything is said and done
I should have stopped blowing out birthday candles before reaching the age of 21.

YOUR PAIN / MY PAIN

A trip for two permitted you to leave your son with me
Though there were some behavior problems assured he wasn't acting naturally
Two days later secretly wishing your vacation was at an end
My continued support for your problems no longer can I lend.

Our eyes first met at the local bus stop waiting for the 8:05
A sheltered life of accepted behavior through sounds of liberation suddenly came alive
When I fell a soft landing was not in the cards for me
My emotions took a count of ten on questions involving his availability.

Despite aches and pains like choo choo trains coming in I took one for the team
Given the assignments of others my attitude became less than serene
Everyone feels so confident dropping their work load in my lap
On the issue of friendship, between us creating a wider gap.

ANOTHER BANK HOLDUP

Already in a bad frame of mind over losing friends without a final goodbye
Eyes wet from the falling raindrops although again ready to cry
Experiencing pain from the spoiled food on my breakfast plate
Accepting middle of the line privileges along with others having to wait.

Arriving after me the old woman maneuvered herself to the front of the line
So many transactions perhaps thinking no one else would really mind
The lower torso so stiff when stationary far too long on this cold gray day
Tired blood affects your mobility when the opponents of exercise have their way.

Receiving a well rehearsed sales pitch from another teller behind the glass
Offering forth a personal smile of resignation; this too shall pass
Saying a quick hello to my true friend now on the run
Ready to pay homage to the old woman at the head of the line still having fun.

Whose Mail Is It Anyway?

Pieces of good intentions arriving on a continuing basis
A good credit rating finding a home in a private dwelling oasis
Human hands acting as a shredding machine creating additional waste
Destroying the fiber of a positive thought delivered in good taste.

Another piece of mail with a window arrives at the scheduled time
Blocked from the ownership of the regular recipient like a cutting machine on a dime
Hearing rumors of possible calls the pieces slowly come together
Three weeks after the fact make this a financial night to remember.

Through the phone a late apology is extended to the credit geru's of most high
Explaining the facts behind the false ruse the money people would not allow to slip by
Mutual understanding is now a gift enjoyed by all participants in this ongoing game
A reputation in good standing must be maintained at all costs just the same.

Destination: New Jersey

An early rising for another action packed day
Knowledge of a manufacturing work element again put on display
A tank full of gas and my vehicle is ready to roll
Hoping to face few obstacles this morning beyond my control.

A bumper to bumper scenario so ready to accept that
Outside breezes on the highway keep me from dozing off where I sat
Arriving in town local construction keeps me going around and around
Isolated from my student body and their collective unhappiness sounds.

Through the front office door a man with a clipboard has a smile upon his face
A sign of relief that I arrived safely at his place
A pile of paper along with anxious faces ready to learn
Time to get the class started with no remaining bridges to burn.

A Gentile Reminder Of Unpleasant Yesterdays

The silent assassin appeared at the counter out of the mistic dawn
After nearly three years her demeanor indicated she had done no wrong
Focusing upon the TV I pretended her presence not to see
After a few minutes she publicly identified me.

"Why have you not ventured in the direction of my pad at all?"
"Our determination to ruin your reputation in scope very small"
Responding to her words I placed the blame clearly on her table
Fainting ignorance she declined to assign me a permanent label.

A few words on retirement came forth from the main witness of my foe
How hard they tried to break me to make me let go
The passage of time makes the silent guns of reason appear so
In isolation they continue their game; how little do they know.

The Attack Upon Ma Barker's Bakery

Voices from the heavens like raindrops fell down upon Slim
Calorie control had now created a new waistline for him
Additional holes in the belt as the ounces just melted away
Rumors in the crowd circulated his availability come Saturday.

Ma Barker's pastry section offered sugar in many shapes so divine
Cakes, cookies, and strudel caused diet ideas to resign
Boxes were opened as free samples blew off the roof
Sugar addiction triumphed over good health in the form of visual proof.

Now the voices of sensibility are silent once more
Sweet smells of Ma Barker have advanced to the center core
Fat layers and heavy breathing are back again for all to see
Continuous chest pains now added on as another later life disability.

A CONTINUING SOCIAL DILEMMA FOR WOMEN

Two opportunities sitting comfortably at the bar
"What are my chances this evening for romance to go far?"
Tired of spending too many lonely nights alone in my room
"Will good fortune be mine on a night of a full moon?".

The cool one offered to buy me a drink
His worldly phrases and fast lines put me in the pink
A red flag appeared when he offered to show me his house
Just another notch on his belt for the adorable louse.

The other one not drinking liquor quickly put me at ease
A responsible person so eager to please
A sense of humor inside of him unable to find
His level of predictability for a blind woman so boringly kind.

Going home mentally comparing social notes inside my head
The best and the worst of the male social animal it has been said
Not willing to continue allowing lonliness to get the best of me
Neither applicant my complete idea of a prince in the galaxy.

A Look Back Through The Eyes Of A Baby Boomer

Peace in our time a little over a year old
Pesky's hesitation cost the Sox dearly I have been told
The spirit of Thanksgiving manifested itself from coast to coast
Meanwhile a premature birth in Newark signaled a defining moment for a toast.

Wearing a patch over my left eye where surgery was done
A young slugger in the midst of a Triple Crown Season was having a lot of fun
Whiffle ball and stoop ball ever the main components of my desire
Another time for the "I Like Ike" political slogan to stroke the political fires.

During the third year of advanced education falling victim to a bad choice
Months would pass by before I found a strong voice
Going private for my sanity became the best thing
Thirty three consecutive zeros in the fall classic produced a hollow ring.

Happy Birthday Uncle Sam with two hundred candles upon your cake
Another year of health issues my redeeming fate
At the end of the year a chapter would close
In the near future on my own like the scent of a fresh growing rose.

Settled in without fanfare on my government seat
Handling all cases; the strong and the weak
The attitude crew from Shea produced the greatest comeback of all
Future Super Bowl Champions from the Meadowlands too were having a ball.

Saying goodbye to a true love of my life
An act of hesitation ended all chances of calling her my wife
Half a century of living how little did I know
In the future besides my waistline would my intellect ever grow?

Losing hair while passed over by the ladies again
Maybe a worker at the library might call me a friend
Without my father passing down a road called retirement lane
Outside of school textbooks; learning the hard way through sorrow and pain.

As He Fades Into Yesterday

Seems like a long time ago our futures merged as one
Everything about him suggested personality, consistency, and fun
Friends from both sides marveled at our degree of togetherness in the open air
Speculating freely upon the happiness in the future our mutual interests would share.

In opposite directions slowly ever so slowly our unity began to drift away
Small differences in scope became larger distractions as egos had their final say
Adrift in isolation through a sea of tears no saving remedies appeared in sight
Sadly under great stress with remorse I bid our relationship a painful final good night.

With reluctance taking small steps I venture to look back into the past no more
Experience gained through the presence of personal pain now part of my social lore
Taking more time now not hooked by the comic actions of suitors many
A wiser mature woman now relates confidently to her own assets so plenty.

Commentary On The Bicentennial

The greatest hope of mankind two large candles upon the cake
A continuing dream of freedom in captivity not willing to forsake
Ships both large and small up the river they sail
Letters of appreciation already written ready for the mail.

Speeches forthcoming from dignitaries essays written by school children as well
A small dose of freedom collects everyone forever under their spell
Patriotic songs are sung in honor of that hot Philadelphia day
When the Founding Fathers let King George know his mastery over the colonies was withering
away.

Meanwhile in a small town in Columbia another birth was about to be
A young female child completely isolated from the festive tone of democracy
Over the years sympathetic voices pointed her along the path
To the nation of opportunity where men like Washington and Jefferson once sat.

Waving a flag her voice in unison with others upon the lawn
Repeating words one never tires of the birth of freedom's early dawn
Determined to serve her adopted country to leave her mark upon the land
In the spirit of unity when in need respectfully asking for a helping hand.

"Oh bureaucratic overlords catch me gently inside your safety net
Coming upon difficult times since the first time we met
Hear my story, keep your word, help me mend with time
Like the Founding Fathers our common future so miraculously entwined."

Every Road Leads Back To You

When we first started not really knowing me at all
After the smoke cleared making the right call
Not really flashy since consistency is my game
After all the other men finding out I'm really not the same.

Caring enough to make a difference after learning I was sick
Elevating me from status quo to a first round lottery pick
Bringing me coffee thus keeping me awake in the morning air
Listening to my tale of woe showing that you really care.

So many other women blessed with beauty yet hollow on the inside
Your all around potential a sign of personal pride
Among so many pretenders in action a person special and true
On the major highway called life every road leads back to you.

General Lee Returns To Gettysburg

Two years removed from the scene the sound of the trumpets summon you again
A total stranger in a sea of conformity scarcely a whisper viewing you as a friend
Pledged to the cause of isolation though overtures may come your way
Battle tested upon the field of conflict knowing now how well my adversaries play.

Resigned to this challenge though I preferred never to see it come to me
One only learns from the trials of yesterday known to all now as ancient history
If only I could turn back the clock to make the wrong moves right
However in the process of late development finally learning how to fight.

Tears once shed over my losses now flow freely amid an atmosphere of joy
Standing firmly upon my own two feet no longer a scheming woman's Cracker Jack Toy
Waiting patiently to see what happens no longer a hidden mystery
In spite of all the turmoil resting comfortably where I want to be.

Husbands / Boyfriends

The search for my other half relying on friends plus the luck of the great unknown
Not asking for much; just looks, personality, with a little added muscle tone
Taking the initiative at times then falling back into line
Careful not to step on his ego or else no longer will he still be mine.

Not a trophy for my game room or the object of my manipulative games
Using fairness as a weapon in return expecting just the same
Giving him some space no worries when he fails to call
Trusting him completely or enjoying the benefits of a relationship not at all.

Hoping everything goes smoothly so difficult for my eyes to start shopping around
Displaying great patience at times even when my face wants to offer forth a frown
Peering nervously over the fence at the green grass on the other side
At this moment filled with confidence happy to be along for the ride.

I Wonder How He's Doing Today

Growing up in the same neighborhood our paths crossed many a time
When apart we communicated frequently when a local call was only a dime
Dances, picnics, and drive-ins all part of the local scene
Years later on my curiosity scale; "What did it really mean?"

My former love went on to college determined to leave our little town
Determined to see the world having no future by staying around
Meanwhile I specialized in retail at a woman's clothing store
Finding my talent in cosmetics located conveniently near the front door.

No letters in my mailbox; no cards come Christmas Day
The price of our mutual separation a lifetime of regret to pay
After our final goodbye never realizing the heavy social debt
My sun of happiness, once shining brightly through the horizons, had permanently set.

Initial Contact

Watching your steps intently from my viewpoint across the street
Offering a sincere salutation my voice rising to its peak
Turning your head you reluctantly catch my eye
A number of options afforded you concerning the much older guy.

You may reply without breaking stride
You may ignore me having issues to hide
You may cross over and begin a fact finding inquisition
Finding out that despite my appearance I have a sweet disposition.

As days go by the verbal bombardment may increase
You may choose navigating another route to increase the peace
A bonding process may develop as we discover common thoughts to share
So secure at this stage of your life you really may not even care.

Local Pit Stop

Female titans giggling inside their four wheeled mechanized caboose
The inhabitants of their destination completely unaware they are on the loose
Pushing buttons on their cell phone to spring a big surprise
With approaching darkness this local visit limited in size.

Telling family members about their future plans overseas
America alone not big enough for their dreams to please
Fighting off local overtures of food and drink
Snack foods over the last several years have kept them in the pink.

One titan has a tan plus a cough to share with all
The other has stitches on her foot an error of restaurant protocol
After some special moments with final hugs and kisses silently on their way
From the days of diapers now at 21 a prominent role to play.

LOVE DOESN'T LIVE HERE ANY MORE

Your facial expression pleading for forgiveness just like before
This time my mind is made up as I escort you to the door
In the beginning attracted to your manliness now acting like a little boy
Once a couple united now reluctantly used as your personal love toy.

As a woman along for the ride I wanted to grow
While occupying center stage on the sidelines you had other issues to sow
Moving in all directions never following a straight line
You displayed character deficiencies you thought I'd never find.

Carrying additional wisdom I confidently remove myself from the fast lane
Walking slowly in the mode of self analysis with no need for an express train
A visionary process will capture me after loneliness slowly settles in
Looking for a new beginning closing the chapter of regret recently held hostage within.

NO SINCERE DESIRE FOR UNIVERSAL RECOGNITION

A casual observer thought my work skills were worthy of praise
Displaying personal awards of success at one's work station the latest craze
However my conscience wasn't ready to go with the flow
Continuing my personal insistence to be regarded as just another average Joe.

Pushing myself with vigor to get the job done
Shaking my head in disbelief when told about team unity that I'm not the one
Focusing upon a plan of action so narrow and straight
Those pushing other interests always leaving me at the starting gate.

To avoid controversy those in power usually roll their eyes
All bets are off with the work force so reduced in size
No leaders are present where caretakers will do
A difficult pair of shoes to fill when I am retired and through.

One Morning In A Life

Along for the ride with my benefactor behind the wheel
My clothing apparel illustrating my connection with the man of steel
A pile of newspapers balanced snugly upon my lap
Yawning as if to be ready for an early morning nap.

After parking at curbside a solitary sentinel appears at my side
Bringing with him words of encouragement to serve as my guide
Soon safely situated within the food emporium domain
Eager to share daily life experiences filled with laughter and pain.

Emptying the bread box than on to the coffee machine I go
Filling up a few cups of caffeine as only I really know
Setting up some morsels of sweetness then some muffins so fair
Proving to the customers about their needs I really do care.

Watching as triumphs and tragedies upon the news screen do unfold
Wanting like others to be on top of things not out in the cold
A moment of relaxation interrupted as the telephone rings
Another voice in the morning amid the profit they bring.

Places at the counter and tables filled by patrons with thoughts of food on their mind
Looking over light colored menus or ordering by design
Patrons carrying out food to go or entering inside the door
As the minutes pass on the morning period is no more.

Rebuilding Main Street

A brigade of heavy equipment descended upon our block
Due to the appearance of "For Rent" signs designed to turn back the clock
Cutting up the asphalt top soil level beyond repair
None of the brave pedestrians from unique moments of caution did they spare.

From my vantage point it had the appearance of becoming a slow day
Workers as well as curiosity seekers wandered around in complete disarray
Roadblocks at both ends signified the presence of a grim tale
Confusion rather than normalcy became the main commodity for sale.

Tomorrow a new level of asphalt will come in contact with the ground
A picture in the local paper showing the latest triumph of the mayor's reign will crown
Lost motorists and tourists will once again blend into the main stream
As transportation officials behind their desks on the next major project begin to dream.

Receiving A Free One

Passing the machines filled with consumer delight
A vendor's truck at my front door loaded so tight
Opening the entrance to the castle allowing a merchant of good taste to come in
Loading the empty spaces with tasty cousine as many eager taste buds began to swim.

Again and again together we followed this routine
Till the garden of plenty represented once again a profit making corporate dream
Eyeing me slowly with a growing sense of appreciation
In a small way I made this stop for him an easy destination.

Something from the machine today is on me
I desired something without sugar to fulfill my personal fantasy
Later on I reflected as I graciously sipped my herbal tea
A simple act of kindness reflected positively upon me.

Rescue Mission

His doctor rewarded him with medicine to fulfill his latest health needs
In the spirit of satisfaction the issue of carelessness gathered its seeds
With the package of good health resting securely inside his car
On the long trip back he didn't get to travel very far.

The call for help moved decisively through a cloudy afternoon
One of his rescuers pulled unexpectedly from a union issue meeting room
The emergency twosome maneuvered through traffic to the problem location on the street
Where the common sense genie left the area as car keys lay serenely upon the seat.

Along with moral support other forces arrived to save the day
The opportunity to travel again created sunshine in an otherwise gloomy type display
Back to the office to muster some Friday afternoon work like desire
Come Winter another story unfolds as we throw another log on the fire.

Sifting Through The Ashes At Fenway

The rival armies of the diamond came together in quest of late season magic
When the dust cleared the faces of the vanquished looked disoriented and tragic
In the late innings the mighty arms could not secure outs
Done in by mighty swings producing game winning clouts.

Late season arrivals helped the pinstripe brigade demonstrate their domination
Setting off a sense of off season futility for members of the humbled Red Sox Nation
At the trading deadline a small voice proclaimed reinforcements were not on the way
Like the men at the Alamo the local forces under siege would just have to pay.

During the course of the battle unable to find the strike zone
The new hero for the other side now having little facial hair to comb
The victor at the end almost able to double the score
Those in defeat looking back fondly at the end of season 2004.

Standing Up For The Standdown

The first meeting took place amid initial signs of Spring in the air
Unity of purpose was proposed by several speakers a commodity beyond compare
A large number of homeless assisted in many phases under one roof
To those who doubted our resolve here would be displayed our sincere proof.

On the morning of our firm resolve words of confirmation began to disappear
Empty tables offering services confirmed our greatest fear
The homeless were waiting camped outside our front door
Their numbers had decreased like never before.

Those in attendance passed through with hardly a glance
Shaking their heads in disbelief on giving Uncle Sam another chance
Volunteers defiantly pushed forward their fight song "What's In It For Me"
A sense of duty toward the less fortunate was not really meant to be.

Now with the tables and chairs safely stored away
Publicity on this issue to be buried securely for another six month holiday
The homeless should seek another avenue in search of relief
The price of dedication for success of this venue is definitely too steep.

Status Behind The Wheel

Walking through the halls in the early moments of the harvest season
With the arrival of final goodbyes next June there must be a reason
The elite of the institution bond together to create similar futures so real
Feelings of unity and separation coming together behind the wheel.

Not acceptable to walk a few miles to our destination today
Not acceptable to sit inside a rusty old mechanical fossil with youngsters at play
The ultimatum for my parents; "Acceptance by my Peers"
Unable to take "No" for an answer so immature for my years.

The costs of this operation my parents will gladly pay
Focusing now on a parking space determined to have it only in my own way
Respect from my peers toleration from the old guard
Status rather than the honor roll represented in my back yard.

With Your Passing

Our introduction in the midst of a party of three
With skepticism on my mind; "Could this really be me?"
The interior was special; the power of the motor made you really move
The ownership for the taking if I was in the mood.

Driving carefully to keep everything on an even keel
Transmission problems turned out to be your Achilles heel
In need of local maintenance during the Summer of 98
A stiff back a reward for my labors tempting fate.

Strong on the outside under the hood not quite the same
Pushing aside sentimentality as an intruder in the money game
Soon the tow truck will arrive to take you on your final ride
While all the memories I'll retain hidden safely deep inside.

SUMMIT MEETING

The power behind the scenes established in the articles of the day
Those in the field curiously wondering how they got this way
Our humble dwelling made liveable for inspecting eyes
Our questions for suitable answers trying their experience out for size.

Publicly stating personal grudges or continuously hidden from view
Eyes focused upon our visitors or pretending not to know you
Answers given out subject to future speculation too
Even the leader at the top wondering in private what he has to do.

With the verbal examination coming slowly to a close
Some offered forth intelligence others finely tailored clothes
The evidence in the minds which road will they follow
The results in the making acceptable or rather difficult to swallow.

TALL GRASS NOW COVERS THE PAST

Covered in green a peaceful scene where rival forces once did fight
Spreading death and destruction through force of arms by day as well as night
Now the curious disguised as tourists advance upon the land
To preserve the heritage of our flag that flies so high and grand.

Our fallen heroes through eternal rest leave us values to defend
Observing the international community aspiring to locate those called friend
On solemn days of remembrance notes of pride still fill the air
Demonstrators condemn our government on platforms of freedom for which they fail to care.

Cobblestones now buried when above once wheels of liberty and justice found a harvest time
The halls of representative government through special interests now in slow decline
The Founding Fathers created the foundations so many years ago
Asked about their influence today how little the current population does know.

Between the white lines on local diamonds special moments came to be
Now a steel ball of destruction has pushed these memories into ancient history
Looking out through a window survivors silently shed a tear
Memories of success and satisfaction now preserved in a gone by year.

The Battle Against Overindulgence

For recreation my child keeps clicking on his mouse
Able to view anything against the rules of the house
Retaining additional calories as he sits contently in his seat
Concerning outdoor activities with others not willing to compete.

In need of money my teenager acquired a plastic friend
Accompanying him on daily activities like a true Godsend
No matter what the cost always a great thrill
Thinking at the end his parents would always pay the bill.

My oldest rebelled against us creating such a fuss
Not willing anymore to sit with ordinary people aboard a rusty old school bus
Showing her father a model out of a recent magazine
In reply he said "When I was your age I too had this same dream".

For after school activities the library was no longer hip
Ready to hang out with the less studious she deserted the academic ship
Her second home became the various areas collectively known as the mall
Her chances once promising for attending college now so very small.

The Matchmaker

Blowing smoke rings up into the cool late summer air
An unlikely contrast with her styled orange hair
Focused upon by many their gazes but in vain
Soon in a familiar setting observing defendants and their pain.

A latecomer with his gaze wanted to know much more
In the morning hours on the wrong side of the establishment's front door
Asking the impossible of an old man not known for his social graces
Hoping against hope that verbal testimony would suffice instead of changing places.

The guardian of little not willing to give it away
Held captive in his contentment of engaging in child's play
Another patron with years of experience once again forced to go it alone
To capture the heart of the fair maiden seemingly content in her personal comfort zone.

The Pause That Refreshes

Worried about the taste coming out of rusty pipes
A variety of brands at the supermarket to end all gripes
Large gallon bottles delivered to locations by company brand trucks
If your contract expires you're dry out of luck.

Magazine ads push white mustaches of famous people at your eyes
Observing cows in the countryside trying them out for size
Young ones told by their parents how to grow
A happy addition with cookies or cold cereal by those who know.

Leaves from a party in Boston still floating along
An opening act of defiance in the creation of an independence song
Taught by the English to take a break every day
Sharing a bag with a friend means great expenses are there to pay.

Half open eyes long for some caffeine in a cup
An early morning pick me up; for some never enough
Along with some breakfast food, a bagel, or cake
A method that works to keep your sleepy eyes awake.

Heavy in sweetness for those who have nothing to lose
People in disagreement with sugar have to be careful what they choose
A little bit of taste so natural from the vine
The nutrients; a step for healthy living in any health manual one may find.

Little children acting like adults behind a home made stand
Their voices of salesmanship make your money react to their every command
If the taste is too sour call it your own for awhile
Remember the business pro that sold you your glass is just a young child.

All those bubbles upon your TV screen
As you fail another taste test your contemporaries act very mean
Again the big decision between sugar filled and sugar free
Against the wishes of my peer group I choose to remain me.

Bottles in the cellar a real aging gold mine
Your favorite red or white only an expert can find
A small token of thanks for the dinner host
A toast of appreciation accepted by friends from coast to coast.

"Less filling" and "Taste great" have long passed from our medium screen
Cold mountain settings for warm climate seekers just a silly dream
The passage to manhood offered forth at any local bar
A designated driver in any crowd the real evening star.

Putting away a few as a ritual of acceptance in any social domain
Your new friends staggering around so happy that you came
Your body organs fighting a battle against your bottle and your lifetime blues
Your future traveling along any road that you choose.

Stomach problems are controlled by remedies inside your medicinal guide
Held prisoner by overindulgence you cannot go outside
Ice packs, bottles, and glasses available at your side
An answer exists for every ailment for those with wounded pride.

THOSE IN NEED

Battle tested warriors traveling from near and far
Recipients of time honored economic battle scars
A chance to remedy the ills of times out of the past
A temporary mishap for many that seemed to last and last and last.

Services for those with no address to call home
Some in dire need though preferring to be left alone
In and out of medical facilities finally pushed out the door
One solitary day of kindness however unable to even the score.

Some losing jobs finding themselves suffering in desperation zones
Landlords with no conscience reminding them in belligerent tones
Familes divided or united to face these grim realities
With limited mobility often asking the impossible on bended knee.

A select few with no issues joyfully enter the chase
The thought of adding to their well provisioned lodgings their saving grace
Filling their stockings never once feeling any shame
Is this opportunity to help the less fortunate the main reason why they came?

Time Passes By So Slowly

Experimentation allows you to put the pleasantries of normalcy aside
The vicars of good judgement go up against the pressures of peer group influencial pride
Rehabilitation is a long road that removes productive years from your life
Accomplishments are few and far in-between amid the signs of daily family strife.

A young boy going fishing years before becoming a man
Showing off excitement watching a starlet sipping from a Pepsi Can
As a teenager entering a new level of educational school
Young girls showing off wardrobe hypnosis as another educational tool.

Hearing the dragsters making the evening street life come alive
Begging your legal guardian for lessons on how to drive
The high cost of car maintenance allowing others to pay
Following the rules of the road may keep you alive till graduation day.

Following the in-crowd while keeping negative symptoms at bay
In search of false identification so willing to pay
Your grades and your family come under great duress
Remain part of the out-crowd and consider yourself blessed.

Watching governmental leadership so inspirational or architects of the great lie
Seeing others off to foreign countries to sacrifice and to die
The power of the ballot box taken for granted yet desired by many
A democracy without the participation of the people is not worth a penny.

Recruiters visiting local schools seeking out those ready to grow and to learn
A future based upon an installment plan for a select few with idealism to burn
Others may seek an escape route from a small community
While weekend warrior participation offers no guaranteed protection against foreign combat
hospitality.

Your grades or your athleticism may put you one step ahead
SAT scores may put your future dreams nicely to bed
The lords of higher learning may promise then take everything away
Allowing you only a classroom environment in which to participate and to play.

Ugly In The Eyes Of The Beholder

Behind an invisible shield of respectability comes forth a humble face
One not improved upon by the cosmetic industry yet comfortable in its place
A spirit full of contributions allowing judgmental gazes to pass overhead
Determined to voice her ideas sometimes in opposition to what others might have said.

Excluded from social gatherings the prom comparable to the old Berlin Wall
Determined not to lock myself up in total captivity while others have a ball
Joining a club or two as other members lean aside
Holding on convincingly to their material gifts plus their shallow pride.

The eyes of darkness may one day see the light
The true character of the underdog with many ways to fight
"Mirror Mirror on the wall"; not part of my future destiny
Acceptance on the playing field of life is all I desire for me.

Walk With Me Into The Future

Your smile and conversational skills have sustained me for many a day
Traveling long distances for your companionship an expensive price willing to pay
Time to initiate a request to draw you to my side
A negative response my vulnerability not easily able to hide.

Together a cure for lonliness and many other social ills
Together an opportunity to create memories reducing the reliance on therapy and pills
Together listening to words pleasant and those we don't want to hear
Together leaving the past behind us along with thoughts of permanent separation fears.

You alone have the power a magical moment to ignite
You Alone have the power against rejection to put up a strong fight
YOU Alone have the power to create your future destiny
YOU ALONE have the power to see something special in me.

WELCOME TO OUR SHORES

Our doors always open for those in search of freedom and prosperity
Due to issues overseas our nation a long time beacon to balance out inequities
There are guidelines that all must follow to join the freedom party within our home
If there is a problem with our guidelines kindly depart our freedom zone.

To those who are poor, hungry, or carrying another child along for the ride
Quotas have been set to limit the number of applicants seeking to get inside
Paperwork along with patience is the formula for your destiny
Spending time in one of our prisons not a popular choice for those longing to be free.

Our native language proudly spoken by the colonists at Jamestown nearly 400 years ago
A demonstration of bilingual talent for our new arrivals the only way to go
The words of our national anthem in a language now offensive to some
The lives of many sacrificed around the globe in a cause always defended to be won.

In search of political freedom the pride that voting and democracy bring
The opportunity to express yourself freely the core of everything
The ancestors of millions of native born bravely made the long journey to our shores
Not completely happy with our laws waiting anxiously to pass through our doors.

Many feel a tunnel, false documents, or the cargo area of a plane is really worth the trip
Later on openly mocking our authorities how you gave them all the slip
Feeling that present day dangers make the issue of acceptance a given political reality
In the eyes of those who traveled this path before a responsible citizen never to be.

WHEN TEASING BECOMES DISPLEASING

Five occupants laying claim to some space in the same room
Their unique activities in the realm of understanding giving off large doses of gloom
Not really tolerant of individual habits for which they display little care
Secretly wishing that some of their uninvited guests really were not physically there.

Visual scenes lay the groundwork for verbal warfare
Indignities are returned salvo for salvo with little mercy to spare
Combatants may leave in a form of temporary retreat
Only to shortly pass through enemy territory on the return trip to their militant seat.

Beginning a war over a bowl of cold cereal is really sad
With no UN dignitaries present to run up the white flag
The guns of male toleration fall silent at last
An eighteen hour ceasefire will provide peace prize nominators with an administrative task.

ABOUT THE AUTHOR

Stanley R. From has spent his entire life in the state of New Jersey. He has received his BA from Murray State University in Murray, Kentucky; he has received his MA from Seton Hall University in South Orange, New Jersey; and trained to become a school teacher in History. Mr From has spent his entire work career in service to veterans through the Department of Labor for the State of New Jersey.

Mr. From is single.

Everything Else Included is his second book

* * *

I first began writing poetic verse on behalf of my fellow recruits at the Great Lakes Naval Station in 1970. I offered them some verse to impress their girlfriends when responding to Dear John Letters they received in the mail. I took up writing original verse again in 1977 entertaining a fellow tenant at my last location of residency in Irvington, New Jersey

In July 2003 after becoming the victim of a social misfortune that escalated in scope I once again turned to writing as a form of therapy to cure my depression like tendencies. My first book *300 Additional Reasons To Appreciate Me* was the result. Each of the submitted selections in this book represents a story in itself. "I HAVE NEVER ENROLLED IN ANY CREATIVE WRITING CLASSES" Everything written down on paper reflects whatever came into my head at a specific moment in time. My observations reflect a "Tell it like it is" philosophy.

I sincerely hope that this publication will favorably affect public opinion giving those out there some renewed hope in their struggles in dealing with people. Those in a group representing the power of the majority SADLY OFTEN UNDERESTIMATE the power of "ONE" residing in the shadows hidden from public view.